Bertha May Ivory

A Cluster of Roses

And Other Poems

Bertha May Ivory

A Cluster of Roses
And Other Poems

ISBN/EAN: 9783337420086

Printed in Europe, USA, Canada, Australia, Japan

Cover: Foto ©Thomas Meinert / pixelio.de

More available books at **www.hansebooks.com**

A CLUSTER OF ROSES

AND OTHER POEMS

BY

BERTHA MAY IVORY

"ANTONIA"

ILLUSTRATED

ST. LOUIS
ENNIS PRESS
1895

ILLUSTRATED BY SKETCHES SPECIALLY DESIGNED
FOR THE VOLUME, BY

CARL GUTHERZ,
ANDRE BOWLES,
PAUL E. HARNEY,
GEORGE C. EICHBAUM,
J. WILTON CUNNINGHAM,
PAUL CORNOYER,
HARRY CHASE,
GEORGE W. CHAMBERS,
EDWARD M. CAMPBELL.

PREFACE.

I T has been said that a preface is permissible only when it acts as a key, opening to the reader the secret treasure-chamber of a book, or revealing to him the hidden spiritual and mental life of its author. If this be true, a preface to the poems of Bertha May Ivory is doubly justified. The noblest beauties of her Muse are veiled, and cloistered in her heart the pure ideals before whose shrines her life, like altar-lamp, burned itself out in holy, hidden service! To lift the veil, to scale her heart's sealed gates, is the sad privilege of the writer.

A study of song, be it just and generous, implies like study of the singer. The bird-song, heard from afar, delights the ear, but not until the bird flies into sight with beat of wing, and play of head, and throb of lustrous breast, does the perfect chord, the complete measure, the rhythmical full harmony, attune hearts to response. Of Bertha May Ivory, alas! there lives to-day her song alone. Death's white wings fold the singer. Her violet eyes are closed in their last sleep; her clear-cut face, her lissome form, are hidden from our sight; her gentle voice is silent; yet Memory lives, and charms we see no more, still hold our hearts in bondage. Beautiful in flesh and spirit, brilliant alike in mind and manner, Bertha May Ivory, unlike the mis-called vast majority, was happily, even prophetically, named: *"Bertha, beautiful and bright."* Thus we knew her, thus we remember her; thus again we shall meet her in that better life which knows not death,—where "loved ones part no more."

Bertha May Ivory was born — all too few years ago — at the beautiful City of St. Louis, Missouri; an ideal cradle for a poet, since here the Past and Present meet and mingle, blending Reminiscence with Ambition, and haloing the cruder charms of progressive youth with grand and honored memories. Of illustrious ancestry, inheriting through her father, the late Hon. John C. Ivory, Anglo-Scotch blood of royal Stuart origin, and the tact, and grace of *la belle France;* from the maternal side both Irish wit and Spanish charm and beauty, — Bertha May Ivory, nevertheless, was a true

American ; her patriotism a heritage from two great-grand-fathers and one great-great-grand-father, — distinguished officers in Washington's valiant army of the Revolution.

The childhood of this apparently favored daughter of fortune was cradled in a beautiful and picturesque home, to which her reminiscent verse, " A Cluster of Roses," is our Sesame. In this paradise of poet-youth,

> " *The sun wore an added glory,*
> *And the stars shone as angel's eyes,*
> *And the moon was a symbol of Mary,*
> *Whose light led to Paradise."*

Knowing the gloom that overcast her after-years,·one is tempted to linger with the poet-child in her heart's glad springtime, when

> " *Life was a beautiful meadow*
> *Starred with the flowers of youth."*
>
> *   *   *   *   *   *
>
> "*And peace and hope and gladness*
> *Shut out all shadows of care."*

The records of ·her childhood, perhaps because of its happiness, are few. Over the gray old rock of Life, smiles come and go like sunbeams. Tears alone, like storm-floods, make impress as they fall. Hence, we are constrained to pass from the sunlit youth we knew not, to the shadowed girlhood we knew. Upon her cloudless pathway Death darkly swooped, snatching away both father and brother, and the dual blow was followed by sudden loss of all most intimately associated with the beloved dead. The delicate, sensitive young dreamer of dreams and seer of poet-visions, outcast from her Paradise of roses like Eve from Eden, found her tender youth set face to face with an unknown world of practical needs and human struggle : a bleak material world whose roses are few and far between, whose thorns are sharp and many.

Bertha May Ivory won the rose-crown, but not till the thorns had wounded her. Yield her not only the laurels of the poet, but the bays of the victor. Hail to the heroine who bravely hid her wounds! Pride was hers in royal measure ; but still more unquestionably the nobler traits — passionate in their intensity, of Love and Loyalty. Self-sacrifice was as nothing to her : self-immolation little. Against her natural yearnings for the leisure and luxury which were her birthright, the social sphere which was her heritage, and for whose triumphs she was irresistibly equipped ; against distaste of the Real, as slayer of the Ideal loved of poets, — against weariness of responsibilities overburdening her frail young shoulders ; against difficulties and discouragements under which weaker souls must have fainted, she bravely battled,— enduring, resisting, conquering, not for her own sake, but for the sakes of those far dearer than herself. Her "Queen," the "brown-eyed, silver-haired" mother she idolized, and in whose honor some of her tenderest songs are sung; the fair young sisters with whom more than one verse acquaints us, these were the beloved ones for whom she strove and triumphed.

> "Would, my own, that I could smother
> With my love, the pain you bear!"

Such was the ceaseless cry of her unselfish heart, the sateless desire, the single aim of her youthful life, whose loving and lavish filial, fraternal, friendly service was faithful unto death!

The true, the selfless, the heroic, these the gods love. Alas for us who mourn her,

> "Whom the gods love, die young."
> *   *   *   *   *   *

The life-work of Bertha May Ivory—inasmuch as it is ended, even in its fair beginning—is difficult to review. The notes of a lark on the wing, the hues and tints of butterfly-wings in flight,—how, justly, may we judge these, hearing not the song to its end,—catching but a glance at beauties blended as they pass us? Bertha May Ivory's pen was like herself, impulsive, versatile, vivid, brilliant! As a journalist, her career, even in its brevity, was phenomenal for youth and womanhood. Her ability was remarkable; her promise such as years must have fulfilled. She was ready, reliable, ambitious and courageous. Much of her best work in this sphere was necessarily anonymous, and hence unrecognized by the public; but the respect and support of a conservative press prove its true value, and over the signature of "Antonia" she wrote herself into the hearts of the people, her relinquished pen being missed and mourned by many an unknown friend. As a writer of sketch and short-story, she was successful in her comparatively few ventures in these directions, as only the young author "born not made," can be; as the appearance of her prose in the columns of leading magazines and prominent literary and social journals attests. Yet it is as a verse-writer, pure and simple, that we must study her most sympathetically, if we would put ourselves in touch with the heart of her life-work.

It cannot be denied that the pathetic melancholy of the greater number of her poems is what first impresses us:— the desperate melancholy of Youth which knows no hope—of Innocence which holds Pain deathless, Regret eternal. But recalling her early lessons in bitter bereavement and misfortune, and the sacrificial life thereby entailed who can wonder if Youth's blithe waters swerved at their turnpoint from banks sunlit and flowered, into gloomier channels shadowed by cypress and rue? Riper life would have brought her consolation ; recompense, if not oblivion. As it was, Death found in her chastened heart at least resignation, born of the Divine Faith whose spark burned in her pure young soul, till it flamed at last into the beacon-star which lit her way to heaven. The steps by which she mounted towards the light, are evident in her verses. Here is her midnight requiem :

> *" Out, out, where cold winds sweep my colder soul,*
> *And knife-edged blasts cut keenly in my heart,*
> *Where shines no star above the sullen clouds,*
> *There shall I watch alone, our love depart."*

And here her psalm at dawning :

> *" I am fearless of the future :*
> *With God's promise in my breast ;*
> *As He giveth storms and battles,*
> *Shall He surely give me rest !"*

Hence the minor chord, after all, was but briefly dominant. The rare chastity of her heart-songs over-rings it like angelic voices. Truthfully she sang :

> *" My love too pure for passion's reign,*
> *'Tis love, and love alone !"*

Her pure ideals and noble standards undertone it, like strong, sweet, golden bells :

> *" I would not choose for wealth of kings,*
> *The pathway you have trod ; —*
> *And stand, as you must stand, some day,*
> *Before the throne of God !"*

Note the holy hope of her many devotional poems ; the graceful sentiment of her happier love-songs, of which "A Mon Bien - Aimé" is a notable example. Mark the glowing enthusiasm of her eloquent tributes alike to noble living and honored dead ! Some of these, especially those inspired by religious fervor, are almost martial in their character. In the stirring lines, for instance, entitled "Ad Majorem Dei Gloriam," who can be deaf to the hint of rhythmic drum-beats, and the measured tread of feet?

And just here must be remarked the loyalty of soul as well as of heart which inspired much of Bertha May Ivory's most earnest work. Her splendid journalistic tribute to the Christ-like work of the Sisters of the Good Shepherd, lives and bears fruit to-day. Her life of Archbishop Kenrick, entitled "Fifty Years a Bishop," won her alike the palms of Church and laity. Her poetic tribute to the dead poet-priest Rev. A. J. Ryan ; sings alike in his honor and in her's. She had the "courage of her convictions ;" and more, the enthusiasm

of them. Let us, with human voice, echo the words God hath surely spoken
to her : —

> *"Well done, thou good and faithful servant!"*
>   *   *   =   *   *   *   *

Lights out! The church bell tolls the hour of darkness. Bertha May
Ivory's life and work and death,—even to this poor summary of them,—are
consummated. What is their issue?

Over the dark and silence hearken the watchword,

> *"Midnight, and all is well!"*

"Midnight" with us, whose lives Death's wings have shadowed? "Well"
with the dead we love and mourn,—God grant it!

Minnie Gilmore

NEW YORK, July, 1894.

INDEX TO POEMS.

INDEX TO ILLUSTRATIONS.

Like some stately ship.

With bright rose-color resting on the mast,
The ship hath sailed and glided from my life,
With all its freight of joy and love for me.

A Memory. *Page 1.*

Illustration by HARRY CHASE.

A CLUSTER OF ROSES

AND OTHER POEMS.

A MEMORY.

I SIT in thought before my glowing fire,
  And slowly watch the ember pictures rise,
A little child, I hold within my arms,
  A child with angel face, and deep blue eyes.
My hand is resting on her sunny hair,
  A golden frame that holds the gentle face,
She nestles near my heart, a picture fair
  Of childish beauty, and exquisite grace.
"Aunt May," she whispers, in her dove-like tones,
  "Please tell of grandpapa, so dear, so good,"
She pleads so sweetly, that to say her nay,
  I do not think the very coldest could.

Ah, little one! you do not know the pain,
  Your sweet request hath brought my wearied heart,
The waves of memory that dash my soul,
  The bitter grief your asking doth impart,
For like a wall of sable doth arise
  The dreary present, whilst the dear, dear past,
Shines fair and golden, like some stately ship,
  With bright rose-color resting on the mast,
The ship hath sailed and glided from my life,
  With all its freight of joy, and love for me.
And so my darling's sweet request hath brought
  So plain, the woe that follows memory.

1

But then I put all saddening thoughts aside,
 And tell her of my father, good and grand,
And how he would have loved to see
 His little grandchild thus beside him, stand,
I tell her of the happy childhood days,
 The summers, that he took us far away
To where the sea foamed, mighty in its strength,
 And on whose shores we children loved to play,
And how, when winter time would come again,
 The joyous Merry Christmas' we'd spend.
The trees, the jewels, pretty dolls and toys,
 Which he would tell Old Santa Claus to send.

This pleases her, but soon I glance me down,
 The little child lies dreaming fast asleep,
And so I fold her closer, and dream, too.
 But they, alas, are waking dreams I keep.
I see my father, so erect and tall,
 So proud, reserved, yet gentle, good and kind,
With face whose majesty was index true
 Of his high soul, superbly gifted mind.

Life's sky for those he loved seemed wondrous fair,
 The sun then bright, the heavens blue and clear.
But God had willed that we must suffer, too.
 So one dark day we gathered 'round his bed
To feel his dying kiss, and kneeling there,
 Receive the sacred blessing on each head.
I seem to see the solemn, darkened room,
 Where in the midst, he lay upon his bier,
So calm, and peaceful, like a king in death,
 Whilst we stood dumb and could not shed a tear.

The dark, thick hair, with but a tinge of gray,
 Lay soft above the noble, lofty head,

And strange, but on each cheek was seen
    A faint rose flush. He seemed asleep, not dead.
The flowers, white and rare, that friends had sent,
    Seemed as if breathing sorrow for the dead,
The waxen candles shed their luster dim,
    Upon the crucifix above his head.

And then, at last, when he was laid to rest,
    And we were left without that father's guide,
What bitter sorrows, and deep griefs we had,
    That we had never dreamed of ere he died!
My heart is weeping, and my eyes weep, too,
    The tears are falling on my darling's face.
She starts, and opens slow her starry eyes,
    That glow like sapphires in an ivory case,
She, scarcely knowing why, is weeping, too,
    I stoop and gently kiss her tears away,
And dull my grief, and try for her sweet sake,
    To force a smile, and seem more bright and gay.

Absorbed in thought, and memories of the past,
    I quite forget the dim, fast dying fire,
Until I start and see the last small flame,
    Like some wild hope, leap up and then expire
A few dull ashes, growing cold and gray,
    Are all that's left of fire pictures bright,
And so it is, alas! with Life's best joys,
    They burn awhile, then fade away from sight.

FOR THE LAST TIME.

FOR the last time my own! It cannot be,
　　We two shall stand in love's communion sweet
Never again, nor moonlight pure and pale
　　　　Shed proud cold gleams in bars athwart our feet,
　　　　　　For the last time.

For the last time, beloved, the stately fronds
　　Of calm, cool palm, and warm rose banks bend near
To us in silent sympathy of sweets :
　　　　Love dies when once his lips are touched with fear,
　　　　　　For the last time.

For the last time, we dwell in blissful trance,—
　　The dream in life, the life in midst of dreams,
Be ours, for that was summer's golden sweep,
　　　　And then beyond lurks drear December's gleams,
　　　　　　For the last time.

Moonlight and roses, pale and ruby glow,
　　Their path colliding ours in blissful reign,
Love and his arrows twined in knotted peace,—
　　　　Love and his subjects, happy slayer and slain,—
　　　　　　For the last time.

Winter and snow, beloved, must come to us,
　　Chill shafts of ice, where flowers decked our way,
Summer but sped in joyous, sparkling flight,
　　　　But winter comes, and comes alas! to stay,
　　　　　　For the last time.

For the last time, again I breathe it dear,
    Rest here within mine arms, and raise thy face,
In faultless.loveliness, to touch my lips
    With all the pathos of Love's dying grace,
        For the last time.

CONQUERED.

S HE pushed the dark hair from her pallid brow,
    Her weary eyes regained a lustre clear;
She rose, and cried: "The stormy fray is o'er,
    I cast afar the cowardice of fear!
Those noble ones, who conquered, not as I,
    Did feel the pass oned thrill of love divine
Never! Or else they'd brave the depths of Hell
    To feel its rapture, quaff of its red wine!

"Duty, the calm, pale coward! I have fought
    With it too long, gainst Love, with crown agleam!
Nay, it shall yield, unto my burning will
    And fall asleep, like some white, ghostly dream.
I choose, dear Love! Too long I've battled 'gainst
    Its poppies slumb'rous, its thrilling wine.
On, to caresses where his soul shall melt,
    And fuse into a single soul with mine!

"On, to his kisses, steeping in their sweets
    My very heart, and drugging life to sleep,
Until all else forgot! Fool, that I've stayed
    So long, to teach my soul to watch and weep.
        Love, I will come!"

Fevered, abright, she passed — the battle o'er,
    But, as she sought the lotus-land, her eyes,
Fell on a picture pressed against a wall —
    A figure 'neath Jerusalem's leaden skies —
A form where lance had left its gory thrust,
    Where thorns to blood had pierced the grand God-brow—
A naked form clasped to the cross, with nails,
    The hue of death that sealed the Savior's vow.

Frozen she stood a moment, gazing there;
    Then with a tearless sob, upon her proud knees fell,
Without, the wind howled like a tortured soul,
    And seethed, and moaned. With every rise and swell
Low drooped her head; then, raising her deep eyes,
    Cried: "Let me bear Thy crucifix O God,
E'en as Thou'st died for me, and let me bear
    However hard the smiting of Thy rod!
      Duty, thou'st won!"

FOR THE FIRST LOVE'S ALWAYS BEST.

SHE came to me in a careless way
    And idly spoke thy name,
I over my 'broidery bending low,
    Felt my face leap to a flame.
And the dainty bit of my lace-work swayed
    And dropped from my finger-tips,
My teeth closed over and nearly pierced
    The depths of my trembling lips.

I thought, beloved, that I had forgot,
    And one day in the long ago
Had buried thy face in my heart's ravine
    And covered it over with snow.
But to-day when she spoke in a careless way
    The snow-drifts swept afar,
And out of its lonely grave thy face
    Shone forth like a changeless star.

And my tears washed the present and real away
    The past flashed back Love's zone,
And I knew in the circlet of Love and Life
    That thou wert the precious stone,
For Paradise was the loveliest spot
    On this earth, and the May-time rose
Is far more rare to our waiting sight,
    Than the one that the late wind blows.

For childhood's the sweetest time of life,
    And the bird loves his early nest,
And all things tell in the song of life,
    That the first love's always best.
And so, beloved, in time's vast sea
    I may drift on each changeful wave,
But ever, and often thy haunting face
    Will gleam from its sacred grave.

AT THE OPERA.

A BREATH of violets, a mist of lace,
  A star-light smile, on the fair cold face,
A dainty comb in the soft, dark hair,
A gleam of gems on the white arms bare,
A flash of diamonds upon the breast,
Two costly drops in the small ears pressed,
A cluster of flowers within one hand,   .
A fan of plumes at her bright command.
And I watched her afar, with her smiling eyes,
And I saw the glance of her swift surprise,
And I noted the face so calm and cold,
Which never to mortal its story told.

But I knew, my lady, your secret heart,
And noted the flush, and the trembling start,
And I saw the feathers, that creamed your fan,
Sway like an aspen. I saw you scan
With that swift deep glance, one face that came,
And I marvelled if wealth, and your craving for Fame,
Could win such glances from your cold eyes,
Or veil the depths of that glad surprise
Which grew to pain, when the mind's real thought
Crystallized to the grief it wrought.

Ah, you clasped your flowers, my lady, there
And you buried your face, in their perfume rare.
He saw you, too, but I think the gleam
Of those haughty eyes, showed no buried dream.
And I marvel if meeting your eyes, at last,
Yours felt the scorn, from his proud soul cast

The brilliant throng bedecked with gems
Smiled bright as queens in their diadems.
And the gold lights flashed in their garish glow,
And the voices rose aloft and a-low.
And the music swelled, and words sped sweet,
And smiling faces hid heart's deceit.

Ah, well, she sat in her misty lace,
With the star-light sm le on her fair cold face,
And he bent over another one,
Well, this the world and the life we run.
And I thought in the splendor of opera glare,
Of one sweet night in the silent air.
There were no feathers, or frosty laces,
But two different smiles on two different faces.
Que voulez vous? What a world is this!
And griefs pain most, n the midst of bliss.

MY FAITH.

L O, the crystal globes of hope, creep
    Sweet, athwart my stormy breast,
And the glass swift melts, to liquid
    Drops of dew to bring me rest.
Am I tired of the conflict,
    War of world and love and strife?
Am I weary of the tempest,
    Equinoctial w nds of life?

What if rains from sorrow's torrent
    Wildly dash across my mind!
What if clouds of sullen ebon
    O'er the sapphire skies I find,
Still the stars are hiding gently,
    Neath the clouds, however black
Still the Queen Moon's stately splendor
    Not one lustre-light shall lack.

Stars and moon are iridescent,
    Rainbow cluster 'neath the sky,
Emblems sweet from Angel Hopeland
    Flash their beauty ever nigh.
Why despair? The blackest storm cloud—
    Must perforce sweep past some day;
Why repine? God's promised splendor
    Changeth night to smiling day.

Yet the clashing chains of anguish
    Like hot iron press my breast.
And the fetters gall and wound me
    Till I sob and plead for rest;
Till I dash the chains to break them,
    Feeling captive all too strong,
Till I try to spill the poison
    Of this earthly grief and wrong.

Peace, the poisoned cup untasted
    Shall change into sweetest wine.
Bear the heavy iron fetters,
    They a flower chain shall shine,
I am fearless of the future
    With God's promise in my breast,
As He giveth storms and battles
    Shall He also send me rest.

He will try me, ah, not ever
　　Far too deep beyond my strength,
When the burden groweth crushing,
　　He will say : " 'Tis spanned the length."
He holds always out that gentle
　　Tender hand to guide me true.
In the vista of earth's tangles,
　　See I Heaven creeping through.

TIRED.

CROWN me memory to-night ;
　　Lay not roses at my feet
From which life and beauty's fled
　　Dead, but ah, so sweet!

Ah, those roses, with each breath
　　Fragrant, spite the dear, dead heart!
How they cloud my soul with pain,
　　Hopelessness impart!

Wild regrets, undimmed by tears
　　That have scorched my soul—
Dreams too vivid, in their strength
　　That thou dost unroll.

I am tired, and I pray
　　That thy anguish cease.
Fling not roses at my feet,
　　Crown with stars of peace.

Dear dead roses! Brush their leaves
　　From my wearied sight;
Let me wear the lilies' glow,
　　Memory, just to-night!

LOVE'S MAGIC GIFT.

TWO little Loves with golden heads
    Went forth in early morn;
They passed a woman proud and cold,
    Who turned from them in scorn;
But yet they loved the woman fair,
    And one bright little Love,
To please her, took the diamond star
    From off his breast—above.

He reached, held out to her with smiles,
    A sparkling, glittering gem.
"Leave me!" she said, "I want it not;
    My soul is sick of them."
Drooping, the cherub sped away,
    But, lo! the other one
Went forth into a field near by,
    Where shone the morning sun,

And raising from its fragrant home
    In robe of purple hue,
A dark-eyed pansy in his hand,
    Back to the woman flew.
With eyes averted, proud, she stood
    And coldly would not see
Until the gentle voice breathed low:
    "I've brought 'hearts-ease' to thee."

Then warmth, like sun, stole in her eyes;
    The flower clasped her breast;
In her proud arms she raised the Love,
    His golden curls caressed.

Poor cherub with the glittering gem
    Sped in the distance far,
And hearts-ease wins a weary breast
    Where fails a jeweled star.

FRAGRANT STILL.

A H ! twilight, thy veil of violet
    Hath come when I need thee most,
To throw round thy misty circlet
    Like some pale, shadowy ghost.

Dropped from a wealth of memories
    I come on a lifeless rose,
And my heart grows faint with languor
    From the fragrance its dead heart throws.

Sad as the mist of evening
    . Ere the moon and the stars arise,
Comes the thought of the time when this flower
    Was dewy as now are my eyes.

Comes the dream of a radiant even
    'Neath the gleam of the stars above,
Comes the echo of blessed awakening
    To the sweet command of Love.

Comes the memory of silver starlight,
    And ah! I can see it still,
The beautiful moon soft creeping
    O'er the crest of the sleeping hill.

And oh! I can feel the zephyrs
    As they toyed in play with my hair,
Chasing the glancing moonbeams
    That smiled from in hiding there.

And midst the deep dark silence,
    Comes the voice that alone would thrill
My soul with its mighty power,
    My mind by its royal will.

And oh! the touch and its power
    Out deep in the silent air;
That first caressing its petals
    Placed the flower to rest in my hair.

Ah tears! It is now before me —
    Bright color and life all gone —
Beautiful blossom once glowing
    There lying so pitiful, wan.

Yet though the brilliance hath faded
    A faint sweet fragrance it throws;
But only two souls know the secret,
    In the heart of my own dead rose.

THE SONG OF THE CYNIC.

ROCKED in the cradle of memory—
  Cradle of memory sway!
Bear me afar to the beautiful realm,
  Bear me away and away!
Carry me back to my yesterday—
  Back to my tropical sun,
Back to the passion, and life and light,
  Let them again be won.

Line the cradle with gleaming thoughts,
  Flowers of Fancy's glow,
Perfume with grace the might-have-been
  In the aisle of the long-ago;
Silver stars, of the twilight peace
  Crowd in my heart to-night!
Flood it with glorious, tranquil rays,
  Shafts of the truth aright.

Cradle of memory sway me now!
  Roses of thought beguile.
Dimples of Fancy, light my soul,
  And crown with a heart-sweet smile!
Bear me away, from the stern to-day,
  Back to my realm ideal!
There is the only rest. And Time
  Press on your signet seal!

Traffic and mart, ye tire my soul,
  Base-born children of world,
Stride in your battle of strife and woe
  Under desire unfurled;

Kisses are cheats, and smiles deceits,
    Words of love are to gain,
Friendship's the only snow of life,
    Love is the storm and the rain.

Fame and glory are phosphor'ent ghosts
    Wan as the air they move,
Grand results are the knells of death
    Hollow the truth they'd prove ;
Bliss is the child of a passion light,
    Joy is the ghoul of naught,
Pleasure is only the price of pain
    Paid ere the debt is wrought.

A wedding's only a funeral guard,
    A feast, but a famine's shade ;
A soldier's, only the groom of blight,
    A widow the echo of maid ;
Men are only the fickle slaves
    Of the passions basely sprung.
And woman only the drift of life
    From the tears of its bosom wrung.

Life, and strife, and pleasure, and pain,
    Mingle, and glow apace ;
Tears are the offspring of idle joy
    And burn on the world's great face ;
Bells, and knells, delight and blight,
    And ballet, and ghosts bestride,
And all these forms of the awful Real
    On the rounds of Time high ride.

In her proud arms she raised the Love,
His golden curls caressed.

There are hosts of ghosts and phantoms gray,
    There are steeds of the grim must-be,
And the River of Life, is filled with strife
    And it flows to meet Time's sea;
So cradle of memory lull me now
    Away from the too stern Real!
Bear me away to my beautiful realm,
    The joy of my blest Ideal!

ALONE—AT LAST.

[Suggested by a copy of the well-known picture.]

ALONE at last! Sweet bride of mine—
    Away from crowded sight,
We two now stand apart in bliss,
    Wrapped in our joy's delight.
The strains of music echo near,
    Rare banks of flowers glow;
The roses' scarlet faces rest
    With lilies' faultless snow.

The voices of gay pleasure's throng,
    Die in the distance, dear;
We two, alone in Paradise
    Of solitude are near.
There on an ottoman is cast
    Thy bridal wreath and veil,
And on thy bosom's throbbing space
    The orange buds grow pale.

Beloved, with thy warm lips on mine,
    Thine arms about me thrown,
Thy fragrant breath, sweet mingling mine,
    In rose-clouds happy blown,
Those brave, true eyes low drooping now,
    Half timid, warm with rays,
Rare passion's sun all sweet subdued
    By modesty's pure haze.

Oh! transports sweet, oh! precious wealth
    To hold thee here, mine own,
To claim that regal face and form
    And best, the soul's white throne.
I love thee, dear, and woe is me,
    That ghosts of what has been
Rise threateningly to taunt me now
    With half forgotten sin.

Beloved, if I might only dare
    To read life's book as thou,
To know each page was snowy fair,
    As thy pure cloudless brow.
But ah, the specters rise from out
    The mists of bridal wreath,
And in the sea-spray of pure love
    Dark rocks rise from beneath.

Away such thoughts! The little hand,
    I held to-night, when deep
I vowed but for one love to live,
    Shall lull remorse to sleep.
That little hand, I vow, alone,
    Shall ever rest in mine
And as we stand, alone at last,
    I swear at Hymen's shrine.

The flowers breathing o'er thy heart,
  The pearls upon thy breast,
Glow not more sweet, nor shine as fair
  As my love's peerless crest,
Thy veil and wreath lie cast aside,
  Sweet bride of hope and grace,
Yet from their snowy mists arise
  Trust's perfect spotless face.

One sacred kiss, the corner stone
  Of joy that ne'er shall fade,
A grand sweet edifice shall spring
  Beneath resolve's arcade.
Droop, orange blooms, in beauty fair
  Thy mission is all o'er,
For thou didst crown a vestal maid
  My queen forevermore.

CHANGED.

THE same sweet book, beloved, to-day
  I held, that often you and I
Have read together with such joy,
  We little dreamed was doomed to die.
Half carelessly I turned the leaves;
  Then flowed emotions' deeper tide,
And o'er the pages rained hot tears,
  With inky clouds the book seemed dyed.

And yet within it, saw I clear,
  Bright mirrored all those golden days;
Again I dwelt within that sphere,
  Bathed in enchantment's rainbow haze.

Again I breathed in radiant realms,
　　High-spanned o'er me the arch of bliss,
And in a rapture scarce of earth
　　I felt the might of Love's first kiss.

I felt an impulse rare and deep,
　　In truth I lived all o'er again;
The Love-god sent his fire-tipped darts,
　　Half wild to tingle in each vein.
Sweetheart, those days are pearls long lost,
　　'Twere vain in yearning to recall,
For on the bier of buried hopes
　　Regret's dark curtain drops—a pall.

Now in our souls, reigns sombre night,
　　And cherished hopes are buried deep,
Though tranquil, from the hand of time
　　The throb of anguish lies asleep.
But, oh, beloved; sweet, precious heart,
　　To think what each to each has been,
And that which comes from Heaven itself
　　To cherish now were but to sin.

'Tis wrong to love, but not to dream
　　Of that sweet time, of youthful joy,
And in the flood of memories, dear,
　　The bitter real we may destroy,
It is not wrong that we have loved,
　　'Twere only wrong to love so, still;
We can but soothe the present's woe,
　　Recalling the past's blissful thrill.

HESITATION.

A STARLIGHT kiss for her, my gentle love,
   Who wore a white rose, in her soft, dark hair,
A pure, sweet kiss, as pure and sweet as she,
   Who wore a white rose, in her soft, dark hair.

A warm embrace for her, my precious own,
   Who wears a wine-red rose upon her breast;
As warm impassioned as the willful love,
   Of her who wears a wine-rose on her breast.

A tender hand clasp for my heart's best friend,
   For her who carries violets in her hand;
As clinging as the halo of her love,
   Of her who carries violets in her hand.

Which the most dear, the fair and sculptured face
   Of her who was so sweet and vestal fair?
(There beat a heart beneath the marble mask —)
   Of her who wore a white rose in her hair?

Or she who wears a red rose on her breast? —
   (Does there a soul, beside the warm heart rest —
Which fierce and pulsing throbs, and passionate?)
   My own, who wears wine roses on her breast.

Or she who carries violets in her hand,
   Dear, tender hand, that soothes with pity grand
Where passion tires, and love grows faint and cold;
   My friend, who carries violets in her hand.

MIRAGE.

A HEART strayed in a garden,
 Breathed wealth of fragrance rare
Blushed bright beneath a rainbow
 That decked the sky so fair.

But soon it fluttered feebly,
 When the fragrance lost its power,
And when the bow grew fainter
 With the dying of each flower

The heart fell in a streamlet,
 Without the garden fair,
And grew so chill it fainted
 In the wave of Doubt's despair.

  * * * * *

It woke one morning brighter,
 As it drifted on the waves,
And sought to reach the garden
 With all the flowers' graves.

It throbbed in trembling pleasure,
 As it saw the garden spring
Up in its former beauty,
 And the bow its halo fling.

It gently reached the shorelet
 From out the streamlet's tide.
But this garden was a mirage,
 And the heart — it only died.

WHICH SHALL IT BE?

WHICH shall it be my heart?
  Answer my soul, in truth;
Which it were best to cherish and clasp
  In the ardent days of my youth,

Ambition or love? Ah, I crave
  Both, with a burning thirst,
And both are hovering near.
  Which shall I turn to, first?

The cup that Glory hath raised,
  Its nectar is sparkling gold;
The froth evanescent I long to quaff,
  Ere the heat of the draught grow cold.

'Twill thrill my being, I feel,
  With the passion its wine imparts;
Oh, the crown it reflects is golden balm
  For a hundred wounded hearts.

Ah heart, you say the draught
  May poison despite its glow;
And, soul, you whisper the crown
  May press till it lay me low.

Then Love, she smiles so bright
  In her robes of gold and rose;
I fain would catch in my eagerness
  One flower she blithely throws

Beautiful Love, she gleams
    So fair, in clouds of light;
But the sunlit one in which she stands,
    Is it drifting to day, or night

And when Love's rose is mine,
    Shall the perfume thrill me so,
That my eyes grow dim to ambition's crown
    Which is tempting me now by its glow?

Yet you say, O heart, perchance
    Fair, winsome Love will pass,
And only the image of what-has-been
    Shine back in my memory's glass.

No, no, such will not be,
    This Love smiles far too sweet;
Oh what, with her in my warm embrace,
    Would I care for the world at my feet?

Yet still, there flashes afar,
    The glitter of Glory's wine;
Answer me, soul and heart,
    Which of the two shall be mine?

Could I not grasp them both?
    You answer, they cannot mate;
One or the other I must choose,
    While yet it is not too late.

Both are but baubles of light,
    Frail as the flower I trod;
Yet either — pure — may be crystallized
    By right, to the honor of God.

FOUND WANTING.

I THOUGHT I loved you. What of that?
    We change our hearts, as well as minds.
Who for a diamond cares as much,
    When in that gem a flaw he finds?

I loved you so, and honored you
    As best and noblest of all men;
I was so happy, that sweet time —
    The world is different now from then.

I think I gauged you by my heart,
    It was so deep, and true, and strong;
I placed you on a pedestal,
    How could I guess that I was wrong?

I crowned you king, and honored you
    With all the holiest trust of youth;
I starred your name, with diadems,
    And gemmed it with the wealth of truth.

I let you in that sacred place,
    A woman's gentle, tender heart;
It swift became a kingdom grand,
    A world exiled from selfish mart.

I was a vassal in that realm,
    I barred out every thought but one,
And high up in its heaven there blazed
    A brilliant, burning, tropic sun.

I loved you once. I love you not.
    Ah, well, these things are strange, I vow,
And stranger still, that love or dream
    Could e'er have been, seems to me now.

Save but for gentle Memory's sake,
    You are to me no more on earth
Than any rose I've clasped, and then
    Found wanting in its fragrant worth.

Yet tender dreams leave ghosts behind
    To follow vaguely with their blight.
Our phantom dream has called, I think,
    Your vision clear to me this night.

You are no more to me, I say,
    Than any gem once fair I saw;
And yet—ah, me! Sometimes I wish
    I had not found the fatal flaw.

A SURRENDER.

I LIFT my plumed cap, and yield up my sword,
    My sceptre is turning to dust;
The mail coat of armor, I always have worn,
    Is broken and covered with rust.

Low-trailing my banner, the lone star is gone,
    My paraphernalia lies there;
A battle was fought, and the utter defeat
    Was wrought—by a rose in her hair.

TRUST.

WHERE is the good of repining and grieving—
  Grieving for what was, yet never can be?
Grieving for bright hopes, now faded and withered—
  Dead ere the fullness of light they could see?

Where is the good of bemoaning and weeping—
  Weeping for youth and its passionate dreams?
Weeping for love that has grown cold and silent
  Though once it illumed life with glorious gleams?

Where is the good of rememb'ring, regretting,
  Regretting the friends who once bowed at our shrine?
Regretting the words of eternal deep friendship,
  Worthless and false as the vows they entwine.

Where is the good of all sorrow and sighing—
  Sighing for Joy's dead dreams and past time?
Sighing for even the blissful sweet chiming
  Of one single stroke from Hope's silvery chime?

Where is the good of recalling, beseeching—
  Beseeching life's mighty and storm angry sea?
Beseeching at least that the breakers cast o'er thee
  May leave thee fair pearls bringing heart-peace to thee?

Alas 'tis in vain all this tear-laden sorrow
  No grieving, repining, or pleading avail
Let the burden of sorrow be ever so heavy
  Let the torrent be strong, we must battle the gale.

Alas 'tis in vain, Oh! then, were it not better
  To bow to the Will that bends all for the best?

To drink with a brave heart the cup e'en if bitter
    To bear and submit to God, trusting the rest?

For the deeper the mist, and the greater the cross is
    And the colder and paler shines life's lonely star,
To the soul that remembers—'tis God who ordains it
    Comes a heaven of joy that no sorrow can mar.

THE GATES UNCLASPED.

THE gates unclasped, the gold aisle oped to her.
    She entered trembling, with her white robe drawn
Across her shoulders, for the winds of fear
    Swept o'er the pallor of the maiden dawn.
With faltering steps, she slowly passed her on,
    And as she went a hand outsped to rest
A glowing cluster of warm roses red
    Above the drapery crossed upon her breast.

In vestal robes, wine-roses on her breast,
    She onward sped, when lo, upon her way
A sudden light burst, brilliant, till with hands
    Beclasped before her eyes, the dazzling ray
She hid, yet blazed it stronger still
    Her veiled eyes, plainly caught the high white light,
When lo, a darkness swept, she glanced aloft,
    Still in the aisle she stayed, but it was—night.

Pallid she stood, in shadowy robes of white,
    All marble-still; the roses red had paled;
They could not live in gloom, in dust they fell
    From the proud heights, so late their fragrance scaled.

MY QUEEN.

WHY tell me of traitors, and foemen to love?
  Why sing me of false woman's wiles?
I am caught in the depths, of two tender brown eyes,
  And chained by the gentlest of smiles.
My Queen wears a crown, of the softest bright hair,
  Like a poem of liquid moonlight,
Which breathes the sad story of Life's royal day
  That was clouded by care into night.

But grief pressed its signet in silvery seal
  That rests like a beautiful crown.
While tears of hot anguish changed in her eyes
  To pearls in their tender depths, brown.
The glance of her eyes is like twilight so sweet,
  Creeping close in the realm of my heart;
And her voice is like morning, so rare and so bright,
  That of day is the loveliest part.

This Queen will be faithful to me until death.
  No fickle, light change do I dread;
And she will uphold me which ever shall deck,
  The laurel, or cypress my head.
Oh, my love is the joy, and the light of my life,
  I never will own such another;
Her beautiful eyes, but mirror the soul—
  The soul—of my silver-haired Mother.

DARK MOMENTS.

[Suggested by the painting of that name.]

POOR Genius, thy head is bowed low,
    With laurels it sure is uncrowned;
And misery stands with spread wings
    Where pain, disappointment abound.
The tangles that twine thy proud soul
    Are threads of small ignoble cares,
Which seem to thy mind like vast chains,
    Robbing Fancy of all her bright airs.

If a peril of death thou couldst meet,
    If a deed of hero's part act,
With pleasure thou'dst stand with brave front,
    But 'tis harder, this battling with fact.
With a soul all on fire inflamed
    By Genius furled close in thy breast,
Whom thou grievest too ardent remains,
    Flies not forth to return thee Fame's crest.

Poor dreamer, 'tis pity in truth,
    When but quaffing of Helicon's stream,
Standing proud on Parnassus' blind heights
    To have rudely thus broken thy dream,
When on canvas portraying thy muse
    Enthroned midst the plaudits of Fame,
To pierce through the fleecy gold clouds,
    The voice of thy creditor came.

Down, down, all thy *chateaux d'espagne;*
    Rose fancies all floated away ;
Down center of brilliant applause
    To the truths of a stern every day.
No marvel the ardent young soul
    Is bowed as in hopeless despair,
When no sapphire peeps forth from the clouds
    And the weight of a storm's in the air.

Ah ! pause not, thus idly to grieve
    Whilst palette and brushes lie there ;
For a mine of rare jewels they hold,
    Tho' flint-crust on the surface they wear.
Have courage, lift high that young head,
    Some day it will wear the reward ;
Fame's laurels shall grace its repose
    Yet in truth these "dark moments" are hard.

A LOVE LEAF.

SWEET, let me take that little hand so fair,
    And whilst I slip the ring upon its place—
The pledge to seal our troth—lift thou to mine
    Thy pure, proud, faultless face.

Behold, the gemmed white hand so sweetly laid
    Within mine own, I raise it to my lips,
And swear life's sun eternal, shall go down,
    Ere my love knows eclipse.

A BUTTERFLY'S AFTERNOON.

*V*OILA, what a fetching gown,
   What a bonnet, just a dream,
And somewhere, you can't just tell,
   There's a hint of violet gleam.
            (What a picture fair she makes.)

See her gliding through the room,
   Pausing for a chat with each,
Just a word or two, not long,
   Yet somehow they seemed to reach.
            (Fluent mistress, she, of words.)

See, her hand slips into clasp
   Of each smiling friend, and lays,
Just an instant, but enough,
   Yet a violet perfume stays,
            (Floating from her scented glove.)

Watch her lift her dainty cup,
   Painted loves, upon its space,
Space as pink as maiden's blush,
   When first love glows on her face,
            (Such a perfect grace she has.)

See her lift the fragile *Sevres*,
   Toying with the fretted spoon,
Ere she sips the fragrant tea,
   In the fragrant afternoon.
            ('Tween the sips she lightly talks.)

She entered trembling, with her white robe drawn
Across her shoulders, for the winds of fear
Swept o'er the pallor of the maiden dawn.

The Gates Unclasped. Page 28.   *Illustration by* GEORGE C. EICHBAUM.

Tea with lump of sugar, sweet,
   And a *soupçon* just of cream,
Or a hint of lemon, there,
   Truly a celestial dream.
      (So my lady seems to think.)

Flitting once again she goes,
   Onward through the lighted room,
Everywhere she leaves a trace,
   Of that subtle, sweet perfume,—
      (She a human blossom seems.)

Watch her sweep into the air,
   Adieu over, to her carriage,
• With a friend discussing now,
   The latest picture, book, or marriage,
      (She a sparkling knowledge has.)

On again to other crushes,
   Till the afternoon is gone,
And the crisp and tingling daylight
   Grows to twilight, pale and wan,
      (Then she gives the order, "home.")

As the homeward route is dashed
   Many a shivering wretch is passed,
Ragged child, and hungry man,
   Huddling women, glances cast,
      (Pleading, but she sees them not.)

In her carriage, wrapped in furs,
   Whirling through the snow-filled air,
Past her church, she tarries not,
   'Tis too late to say a prayer.
      (Surely, too, her duty's done.)

Done till night brings other claims,
    Other gowns, and gems, to wear,
Time enough when Lent will come,
    To kneel with fashion at her prayer.
        (Thus she lightly soothes her soul.)
    *   *   *   *   *   *   *
With that high-bred face before me,
    And that lingering, sweet perfume,
'Twere a traitorous thought to picture
    That fair face e'er in a gloom, .
        (Such a *riante* thought she seems.)

A LOVE LETTER.

TO-NIGHT I saw a girlish form
    Within a darkened room ;
She knew it not, that one without
    Watched furtive in the gloom.
She raised her white arms o'er her head
    And knelt in anguish there ;
About her dewy lips were wreathed
    The tendrils of despair.

I saw her draw from out a case
    A letter blurred by tears ;
I heard her read the words aloud,
    As one whose soul half fears.
She breathed the burning words of love,
    Soft promises of truth,
And all the vows of tenderness
    And passion flame of youth.

She lingered slowly o'er each word,
    That once had made her wild
With rapturous joy and gentleness—
    A pretty, trusting child.
The bliss had passed and girlhood fled;
    One day, in p ace, there stood
A form whose mind by anguish sped
    Swift, to sad womanhood.

She knelt with letter in her hand—
    Poor heart, so bruised with pain;
Yet with firm lips, and tearless eyes
    She read each word again.
She rose and crushed it 'tween her hands,
    And dashed it 'neath her feet,
And then she stooped, and raised it up
    And called it dear and sweet.

She pressed hot kisses on the page,
    Then smoothed with fond caress,
And laid it o'er her breast, and prayed
    The words to soothe and bless.
Poor heart! The thought that she was doomed
    To meet him ne'er again,
Must crush her love, new mould her life,
    Half drove her mad with pain.

She tossed her letter in the flames
    And watched it slowly curl,
Until but ashes fluttered where
    The pages did unfurl.
I prayed as only man can pray,
    That in the fire of time
Her heart would burn the record, sad,
    And live a life sublime.

A RESPITE.

IT is not wrong, love, that I stand to-night,
　　Beside love's open gate in memory's aisle,
And gaze far searchingly adown the path
　　Just for a little while, only a little while.

It is not wrong, that there beside the gate
　　I rest my tired head upon my arm,
And turn from all dull life to my ideal
　　Ah, surely I may have this charm, only this charm.

It is not wrong, dear love, it is not wrong,
　　That through the white gates eagerly I seek
The rose-lined garden strangely quiet now,
　　The brilliant flowers drooping pale and weak.

It is not wrong, that in th' enchanted spot,
　　Beneath my gaze the roses bloom again,
And yon gold-feathered bird uplifts his voice
　　Until each note vibrates my every vein.

It is not wrong, that the warm flush creeps soft,
　　To dye my white face with a crimson glow
Of radiant joy, as though the sun had come
　　To carmine kiss the quiet pallid snow.

It is not wrong, oh, no, it is not wrong,
　　That from the shoals of present I now spring,
And with my face deep buried in my hands,
　　My very soul goes forth on memory's wing.

It is not wrong, oh, love, it cannot be,
    'Tis only memory where to-night I'm cast,
Ah, heaven, the respite soothing and so sweet,
    Could not be wrong, it were so quickly past.

It is not wrong, that clinging to the gates
    Now wide ajar and gazing yearning down,
I sweep the path my feet may never tread,
    I see the flowers my head shall never crown.

Surely 'tis nothing, dear to cling me here,
    While shudderingly I see the ocean's surge
That I have battled roll beneath my feet,
    And marvel I had strength to e'er emerge.

All tremblingly, my arms upon the gate,
    And kneeling by my mirage, Paradise,
I pray to God that He has helped me bear
    And raise to Him my hot and tear-filled eyes.

It is not wrong, that I forgot the past,
    And clinging close peer down the sacred aisle,
To ease my heart I enter not, but gaze —
    Just for a little while, only a little while.

TEARLESS.

AND thou art dead, my own, my love, my life?
    They tell me thou art dead—can'st be?—and I am left
Wounded, and dumb, to live this weary life,
    Where every light is gone, of joy bereft.
Ah! thou art dead! Those eyes so wondrous sweet
    Are closed with heavy lids, from light of day.
No longer passion, soft, entreating, love, again,
    Shall light them as the sun illumes earth's way.

I see thee as thou'rt lying, now, so cold,
    So silent, with thy fair hair clustering o'er
That noble brow, like some proud marble dome;
    The temple's crown, alas! soul-lit no more.
In vision I can see as tho' 'twere real
    The smile, half faint, upon the cold dead face;
The gentle mouth, so cold, and firm withal,
    Enwreathed in death still with imperial grace.

And I can see that quiet, still white form
    Lie calm, with folded hands across the breast
That in this life, beat with impulses grand,
    That battled for the right, and conquered—Rest.
Around you I can see the clustered group,
    The ones who have the right to mourn and weep;
They can have tears to comfort—I have none.
    Only my soul, and heart this vigil keep.

These too, these rightful mourners with their tears,
    Warm for the time perhaps, can bend thee near,
Can kneel beside thy bier, can kiss thy face.
    Smooth the soft hair, of one so loved and dear.

But I must stand apart where I can gaze
    With eyes as cold as any stranger there,
Must stand apart nor mingle with the few,
    Those the world says, have only right to care.

They weep! Ah, God ' if I might only love
    So little, that my grief might find, like theirs,
In tears, some thawing of the icy band,
    Some loosening of the barb that wounds and tears!
Tears, angel tears, are all my cries in vain?
    Will you not gather like the pearls that rise
From ocean's depths, tossed by some angry storm,
    To ease my heart, and clear my burning eyes?

And yet, why thus! For my own love is dead,
    Surely, in Death, at least, he can be mine!
Surely, the fate that rose like some black strand
    Must die with Death! Life's claims no longer thine.
Mine, mine, tho' thou art dead, the bliss to feel
    That I can steal out, to thy lonely grave,
When others cease to think, and kneel and pray,
    And sink my soul 'neath memory's mighty wave.

And, oh, to-day is not like one that's gone,
    That fearful day of anguish, woful grief,
When thousand arrows odged within my breast
    To stab my heart, and shut out Hope's relief;
Then when I quaffed Fate's bitter, poisoned draught;
    When coldly parted she afar each heart,
I thought death nigh, I knew not how to live,
    But for ourselves, we cannot choose life's part.

God willed it! And I suffered, He knows how,
    And He knows, too the bitter, biting pain

That followed, ere the wound grew partly healed,
  Touched by the ointment, Time. The cure was vain.
Ah, but my heart grew sick with silent woe;
  But rising moons, brought duties to be done
I lived and breathed, I even smiled and sung,
  But like a world that moved without a sun.

'Twas then that I unlearned the blest relief of tears;
  I lived because I breathed, and that was all.
To-day I even smiled, when thou wert dead,
  To know thou couldst be mine, beneath that pall.
And, yet, when I steal out within the night, and see
  The same blue Heaven, and stars that shine above ;
The same Queen Moon, that listened to our vows,
  Th' impassioned transports of a first, sweet love,

And know those eyes will never, never more,
  Shine bright in beauty, as they oft times shone ;
And know those hands shall never clasp mine own,
  Nor that sweet mouth, let fall each gentle tone ;
And know that life is hushed forever, love,
  I here alone, thou 'neath the cold dark mound,
I cannot think, I dare not whisper hope ;
  Ah, Heaven will come, and then thou shalt be found!

ONCE.

A ONCE sweet real 'tis only this :
   A swift hand-clasp, a hasty kiss,
A soft, bright glance, a whispered word,
A spray from out love's ocean stirred,
A moment but of heaven-like grace,
A face bent down to touch a face,
A warm response from each stirred soul.
A moment's rest upon joy's shoal,
A swift unclasping of fate's hand.
A sea, dividing land from land,
A smile of happiness—ah, me !
A nothing now, but memory.

MEMORY'S ENCHANTMENT.

I STAND in the asle of memory,
   'Neath the silver haze of thought,
And a dreamy rapture thrills me
   By a mystic power wrought ;
For the aisle is lined with roses,
   Gold-hearted, petaled, bright,
And their tender lives are breathing
   With a silent, sweet delight.

And throughout the aisle of memory
   Creeps their gentle, damp perfume,
Gleaming with crystal dew drops
   Fallen from fairy's loom.

Oh, they glisten and refresh me,
    Bathe my heated heart in peace,
Rippling like magic love song
    That I fain would never cease.

And reverie's moonlight gleaming
    Creeps down the rose-lined aisle;
Illuming all this kingdom
    Like some radiant angel smile.
Oh! the stars of recollection
    Glow with holy silver light;
One by one they stud this heaven,
    'Till they gem the past's sad night.

Yet, alas! through all this beauty
    At my feet athwart there falls
One shadow deep and darksome,
    That my soul in fear appalls,
Thus I stand in the aisle of memory —
    Part shadowed, part so bright;
But the labyrinth holds me captive
    And I may not leave to-night.

In the aisle of tears and laughter,
    'Neath the arcade of sweet peace,
I stand in half reluctance,
    Yet yearn not for release.

A FAREWELL.

IF we must part then let it be, dear friend,
　　Together, with my hand close clasped in thine,
And with our eyes not meeting, but drooped low
　　To hide, perchance, the tears that in them shine
If we must stand above an idol fair,
　　Though lying now in atoms at our feet,
Let us together dig a resting place,
　　There let it lie in coldness, fair and sweet.

If we must part, dear friend, then it must be
　　In silence solemn as the depths of night.
With heavy stillness, sombre as a cloud
　　Ungemmed by moon or silver starry light.
Whom was it, thou or I ? No matter whom,
　　Has severed from its mates the string of gold,
And brought discord amidst the music sweet
　　That echoed from the harp each heart did hold.

If we must feel that never more again
　　Shall the rare chain of crimson tinted flowers
Twine soft about us heavy with perfume
　　And dropping petals on the passing hours,
Still we must bear the falling of each rose,
　　Still we must bear the golden harp's surcease,
And yet they were so strong, and sweet one time,
　　Crowned by the starry wreath of gentle Peace.

If we must part, stand here again with me,
　　Look down upon the silent harp that lies,
In golden beauty, stringless at our feet,
　　Never again to utter tender sighs.

If we must part, let us together, friend,
    Take those rare roses, strew them o'er the place
Where lies our friendship, cold and statuesque,
    With a wan smile upon its chill dead face.

If we must part, go each upon each way,
    No angry thoughts must desecrate the dead ;
In peaceful silence murmur parting prayers,
    And sway a censer o'er the life that's fled.
With upturned face, our friendship lies at rest,
    The crimson roses crumbling o'er her brow,
The harp, mute symbol, lying at her feet,
    Friend, we have looked our last upon her now.

ON THE HEIGHTS.

LET her wear the crown she's won,
    Golden web, by glory spun ;
Let her wear it, wear the fetter ;
Let her bear it, that were better,
Let her flash with radiant mien,
Proud as fairest ideal queen.
Blame her never, justice grant,
For endeavor courage grant.

High her station, she has gained it,
Fame, and beauty brave sustained it ;
But the seeking, ah, the anguish,
See bespeaking in that languish,
Faced the world's hot war in battle,
Scorning all the bomb-shells' rattle,
Never minding all its storming,
Trusting, finding, glory's charming.

On her pinnacle she's standing,
Crowned with genius all commanding;
Ah, alluring seems her station.
Nay, enduring that elation.
Once a rose bloomed in her heart,
Wealth of fragrance to impart;
Proudly clinging to her life,
Ever bringing peace from strife.

Ah, she cherished this sweet flower,
Loved its beauty, owned its power,
Sweetly wore it, till the world
From her tore it, high up-whirled.
Ah, somehow the rose was taken,
From her heart, its petals shaken;
Swiftly fading all its bloom,
No earth aiding saved its doom.

How she anguished for her flower,
Only God knew that dark hour;
But, alas! the cruel storm
In its pass, swept all life's charm;
Still she's smiling, still she's standing,
Still to fame, her baubles handing;
Reached her goal, and yet has lost,
Tired soul, all tempest tossed.

How her gem, the sparkle tires,
Lost her rose, all joy expires;
Let her wear the crown of fetter,
Let her bear it, that were better;
Well, she feels — her wreath is dust,
Still encircle her it must.
Add applause, join in the game,
Never pause, for this is Fame.

A BROKEN FAN.

I BROKE my fan, the fragile thing,
  Quick snapped just now, within my hand;
Excuse me, will you say again;
  I did not hear or understand.
The fan? No matter —You but asked
  When Charlie, our old friend, I met;
Yes, he was just the same, dear boy
  And, no, he is not married yet.

But is to be, and soon. Ah, yes!
  A beauty? Many think her fair—
But, if you'd just as soon not dance,
  Suppose we step out in the air.
The weather is so warm, you know,
  The lights have such a garish glare;
Without the window, see moonlight
  Is silvering trees, and everywhere.

How beautiful! It's charming here;
  So cool the air. Sit down, I pray.
But see, from out the ball-room comes
  Bright Clarisse Fayre, and just this way;
I'll introduce you. * * * Now, if you
  Will both excuse me I will go
And say good-night to all my friends,
  My head aches dreadfully, you know.

Ah, nothing but the heat, and, too
  This hotel life, in summer light
Is twice as trying as the long
  Campaign in winter; but, good-night!
    *   *   *   *   *   *   *

And so I'm in my room at last.
 Ah, moonlight where I kneel be kind
And flood with peace, the stormy pain
 That burns my very soul and mind.
I broke my fan. He little knew
 I crushed it, as he spoke that name
I thought I'd learn to bear ere this,
 And ashes were but left of flame.

I thought the whirl made dumb my wound—
 The whirl of Fashion's world, I tread—
I thought no more I'd resurrect
 The love I hoped lay cold and dead.
His name, so sudden and he asked
 Of her, and him, so calmly, too;
I hope he did not note my face
 And see the anguish creeping through.

What care I, though? Oh, throbbing heart,
 Be still, as kneeling here I pray
Oh, tired soul, be brave, as you
 Have been since that cloud-darkened day.
The fan lies here, the ivory sticks
 Pale, gleaming, crushed before me now;
He just as lightly broke a heart
 And crushed it in a faithless vow.

A fan and heart, they weigh as light
 Within the world's vast scales, it seems;
And broken heart and broken fan
 Lie here within the moonlight gleams.

THUS EVER.

THE old clock of the world,
  The Sun, pointed the hour
And the pendulum Time
  Ticked slow in earth's tower.

And the four-o'clocks nodded
  And said, "On this morn,
In yon stately chateau
  A girl-child was born!"

Then the flower time-pieces
  Looked up to the sun,
Who gilded their faces
  Till his day's race was won.

*   *   *   *   *

Years after, the old clock
  Still pointed the hour
And the pendulum Time
  Ticked slow in earth's tower.

And the four-o'clocks nodded
  Each bright little head
And said, "In yon chateau
  A maid lieth dead!"

Then the flower time-pieces
  Looked up to the sun,
Who gilded their faces
  Till his day's race was won.

Out of the shadow of thoughtland,
Down through the realm of dreams,
Comes my soul, by a subtle perfume,
Like a breath from heaven, it seems.

A Cluster of Roses. Page 49.   *Illustration by* GEORGE W. CHAMBERS.

A CLUSTER OF ROSES.

OUT of the shadow of thoughtland,
    Down through the realm of dreams,
Comes my soul, by a subtle perfume,
    Like a breath from Heaven, it seems.
Someone had brought near me roses—
    Crimson, creamy and pink—
Placed just where I could see them,
    When my mind grew too weary to think.
And the fragrance stole 'midst my musings,
    And it chased, like a sunlit gleam,
All sorrow, and sad repining
    That had darkened my evening dream.

And, oh, the scent of those roses!
    It arose like an incense there,
Wafting so sweet a memory,
    Bringing a peace so rare.
Not the unrestful splendor
    Left of a dream of love,
With its vain and dim heart-longing,
    And the clinging halo above;
Not of some warm, deep friendship
    Glowing, or passed from sight;
Not of some radiant pleasure
    Cold in its frame of light.

Not of the glitter of ball-room,
    Alight with its passing glow;
Nor of some bright girl triumph,
    Nor a youthful transient woe;

Not of a shadow of glory
    Cast from ambition's throne,
Nor of some rare heart-jewels
    Bright'ning life's circling zone ;
Not of some deep love given,
    Nor of a fair sweet hope,
Not of some vows eternal,
    But of wider and purer scope.

For, oh, the scent of those roses ! ·
    Moist, with the evening dew,
They bring back again so plainly
    Sweet childhood's days to view.
They breathe of the home I loved so
    When roses, rare as they
Clambered in coy confusion,
    Through the graceful garden way.
They tell of the long day over
    When tired of romp and play,
I would nestle beside my father,
    Sweet crown of a blissful day.

When a mother's kisses told bedtime,
    And God heard my evening prayer,
And peace, and hope, and gladness,
    Shut out all shadows of care.
When life was a beautiful meadow,
    Starred with the flowers of youth.
When the only angels that whispered
    Breathed of the perfect truth.
When the sun wore an added glory,
    And the stars shone as angels' eyes,
And the moon was a symbol of Mary
    Whose light led to Paradise.

When the perfume of love made sweeter
    Each day than the breath of May.
When I dreamed not the colors of girlhood,
    Could ever grow darksome or gray.
I will not dwell on the sadness
    Nor the broken links, of a home.
I will only think of the gladness
    Ere a child's feet learned to roam.
But, oh, the scent of those roses!
    Moist, with the evening dew,
They call back again so plainly
    Sweet childhood's days to view.
I will bury my mind in their fragrance,
    Their perfume shall smother unrest,
The leaves shall not fall, I will watch them
    And wear them, like hope, on my breast.

CONSOLATION.

COMES the far off silver tinkle
    Of a hopeful bell to me;
Comes an opening in the vista
    Of the great Futurity.
You are sad, my precious darling;
    Your sweet eyes are filled with fear,
And you say that life is only
    A vast sigh and mighty tear.

And you moan in wounded heart cries
    Of the flight of golden days;
Weep that they have passed forever,
    With their love-filled starlight rays.

Would, my own, that I could smother
    With my love the pain you bear,
Or could teach you hopeful courage
    In the thorny weight you share.

Oh! but this is only sorrow
    That a thousand women feel,
When a swift cessation leadens
    What was once love's golden peal.
But some day life's stage shall sparkle,
    And the foot-lights shine so bright,
That their glitter shall illumine
    Till your heart forgets to-night.

Some sweet day a bank of flowers
    Shall uphold your gentle form;
Some fair day a sky of azure
    Shall o'ershine you with its charm;
Some glad day earth's grandest music
    Shall urge on your youthful feet
Till you reach the goal that's waiting
    In your womanhood complete.

Cease your sadness, pretty sweetheart,
    For your clouds are passing swift..
I can read behind the curtain
    That a prophet's hand doth lift.
Who the prophet little weeper?
    'Tis my soul, the Seer to-night
For I know God's tender goodness,
    And my faith doth lead me right.

So there comes the silver tinkle
    Of hope's lovely bell to me,
And I see a shining landscape
    That shall light Futurity.

FROM THE STARS.

IMPASSIONED the artist sat, before his block,
    Chiselling to form the Ideal of his brain,
Patient yet eager, till the curves that crept
    Into pale beauty, thrilled his every vein;
For lo! beneath the fire of his touch
    The statue grew. Above the regal form
A woman's face, then dimly outlined shone—
    Slowly it smiled, complete in splendid charm.

Proud curved the mouth—proud, yet how calm and cold;
    Voluptuous grace of form, yet pallid white.
"White and as chill as death!" the artist cried,
    "If but my art could give thee warmth, and light,
And bring thee color thou dost lack!—yet still
    High on a pedestal shall gleam thy grace."
He raised it with his strength, but lo! as pale
    As marble image grew his own proud face.

Ah! he had given his warm life blood to gain
    This perfect, yet, oh! most imperfect end.
Still love and fame gave fire into his life,
    E'en as the thrills of wine, with passions blend.
Again, the statue in his arms upraised
    One moment, and the craved-for niche was found.
But small is human will,—together fell
    Sculptor and sculptured to the hard, cold ground.

Pallid the master in death's firm embrace,
    With features fireless, and fixed and wan
In frozen silence, while the statue lay
    In scattered atoms 'neath the chill gray dawn.

A HEART SONG.

A THOUGHT creeps softly over my mind,
    Aglow with a golden light;
Oh! my heart smiles bright, as it feels the kiss
    Of that tender thought to-night.
For oh! it is sweet and wondrous rare,
    And gentle as moonlight gleam
Till a warmer kiss from its glowing breath
    Makes my heart like a sunrise seem.

And a thousand fairies with bended bows,
    Did I call them cupids? I wist
'Twere better name for the tiny guests
    That have crept through my heart-life's mist.
They breathe a name in my very soul,
    Whilst their arrows pierce half with pain,
And the little breaths with their perfume sweet
    Soft murmur an old refrain.

Then the tiny voices are raised so high
    As they sing of one rare gold time,
The echo floats o'er my soul and mind,
    So clear is the bell-like chime:
My heart, it is blushing with very joy,
    For memory shows but its rose-like sky;
Oh, fair Queen Thought, with your fairy train,
    You have kissed a smile, from a weary cry.

Creep closer into my heart, and rest,
    Sway there your kingdom one night at least!
Hold high your revels, of joy and love,
    Where famine has been, be there now a feast!

Ah! just beyond on memory's sky
    The roseate glow turns faint and pale ;
The cloud is coming, I see it's gray —
    Let my heart song cease, ere it grow a wail.

THE PENALTY.

WINSOME Love lay asleep on his pillow of clouds,
    Gold-tinged by the bright burnished sun ;
Slow rocked in his cradle of flowers he smiled —
    Sweet rest after victories won,
He slept, and from court of the royal sun-god
    A mischievous gleam sped away
And glanced upon Love with witchery coy
    As in sweet dimpled grace he there lay,

Then the fair little sun-child was wrapped in repose
    On the beautiful lids of Love's eyes —
Whose dreams being troubled — unusual thing!
    With a tremulous start see him rise.
And how did he punish the saucy sun gleam?
    Why both sleepy hands did he raise
And held firm th' intruder within his soft arms
    Whose coming he greeted with praise.

He snatched up his quiver, as quick as a flash,
    And shot forth a dart tipped with fire
Which lodged in the heart of his victim, and changed
    By magic to musical lyre.
In the midst of bright clouds, close laid on his heart,
    The fast captured sunbeam did hold :
Ah, Love, e'en asleep is a dangerous god,
    And nettles his pillow of gold.

AS HAPPY AS A QUEEN.

SHE clasped her hands in girlish glee
  Above her head's gold sheen
And laughing said, "I am to-day
  As happy as a queen!"
Somehow athwart my heart there stole
  A subtle sense of pain,
Somehow upon my careless mood
  Crept pathos back again.

For in a creeping mist of thought
  I saw two shadows there,
And both were bowed, and both were sad,
  And one had silver hair.

EUGÉNIE.

I saw in vision long ago
  The foremost shadow rise,
Time clothed again her regal form
  In fashion's brilliant dyes.

I saw her stand with red-gold hair
  And smiling lips, and eyes,
A queen by right of lofty soul,
  A queen by beauty's prize.
How happy was she queen and wife!
  A child stood by her side,
A noble boy his mother's love,
  A nation's hope and pride.

I saw another figure stand
  In stately grace, he smiled.

Less for the sceptre in his hand
    He cared, than for the child,
And for the one he'd crowned before,
    Crowned, smiling happy queen,
Thus saw I in the past's false dyes,
    This radiant blissful scene.

The gold-illusioned days swept by,
    I saw the present stern;
And to the shadow queen my eyes
    In starting tears did turn;
A flowing sable widowed veil
    Lay where the crown had done;
Still she was not all joyless yet,
    For had she not her son?

But lo! no crown she weareth now
    Save crown of sorrow's tears;
The princely form fades swift away,
    But not the shade of spears.
No haughty form beside her now,
    No smiles upon her lips,
An anguished face, a whitened head,
    A heart and life's eclipse.

CARLOTTA.

I saw the other shadow there,
    Stand drooping, yet she raised
Her eyes n which no light there shown
    Sad, helpless, meek and dazed;
I saw the light of reason gone,
    And memory turn away;
A vacant temple only left,
    Dark night where once was day.

Yet she too clothed her queenly form
    In garments of past time,
And lo! a smiling vision seemed
    Enwrapt in love sublime;
And then a kingly figure rose
    And proud stood by her side,
Oh! far beyond all wealth of words
    Shone out his love and pride.

And then I saw a hand reach forth
    To place upon each brow,
The gleaming circlet called a crown
    That made them sovereigns now.
Illumed by glory, roseate hued
    Ambition's light, and power,
A radiant pair, they seemed.   Alas!
    How brief that brilliant hour.

Again the iridescent robes
    Of past swept from her form.
I saw the shadow queen again
    Bereft of all life's charm.

Naught, said I, to the laughing maid,
    But did not like her words,
For I had rather, she had said
    Her joy, was like the birds,
Of flowers, that bathe in sunlight's wine,
    Or butterflies' gay mien,
But not the words that fell so light,
    "As happy as a queen."

ACCUSED.

SHE bids farewell to Fancy's reign,
  Ah! cherished once so deep,
And now she laughs her heart to scorn
  Because it cannot sleep.
Farewell, she loved you, what avails
  Your passion vows of truth?
You only wrecked a pulsing heart
  Upon the shores of youth.

Be still! No protests, useless vows,
  As light as breath of air.
You chose the world, nor cared you doomed,
  One warm life to despair.
No flowers bloom in all the fields,
  Like thoughts that throng her mind,
No star-eyed daisy blows
  As pure, as soul-refined.

And yet no sun-bright arrows glanced
  More ardent warm, or sweet
Than the deep love she proudly laid
  Low at your careless feet.
With tresses all unbound she knelt,
  The sweetest maid in grace,
And decked the shrine she built for you
  Like some rare sacred place.

She flung her royal gifts of mind,
  Her holiest gleams of soul.
She only wished for your dear sake
  To reach her aimed-for goal,

She laid the treasure of her heart
    Too freely at your throne,
Each paltry smile of yours she saved
    To form her jewelled zone.

And you! You smiled, and called her fair,
    And wooed, and won the while.
And then grew wearied of the wealth.
    One woman's tiring smile!
As base, unworthy of the trust
    As tinted leaves all dead,
Or winds of summer as they pass
    Warm, but too swiftly sped.

Sometime the shadow, too, will fall
    And dim your selfish path.
Sometime the echo of that wrong,
    Shall scorch you with its wrath.
You laugh, no wordly sin is done,
    But love, and trust, and faith,
I say shall haunt your steps, and mock,
    Each an accusing wraith.

No wrong! Are then those kisses naught
    You printed on her lips?
No wrong! Are those caresses dust
    That caused her heart's eclipse?
No wrong! Is shivered, earnest love
    And peace and joy as naught
To weigh within your conscience' scales
    With retribution fraught?
I would not choose for wealth of kings
    The pathway you have trod,
And stand as you must stand some day
    Before the throne of God.

As shallow as a rippling stream,
  With depths of rock and earth,
You won a splendid regal gift,
  And knew not of its worth.
Go, on your way, the giddy path
  Of pleasure and delight!
Go to bright roses, and to-day,
  Forget the stars and night!

Go, think not of the white despair
  That blighted one grand heart;
Yours is a man's allowanced life,
  And her's a woman's part.

AN INVITATION.

A KISS—would you have one?—then steal it!
  For stealing sometime's not amiss,
When it deals in such sweet, airy trifles,
  And yet holds a treasure of bliss.

My heart—would you have it?—then rob me!
  Heart-robbing, is surer than toil.
Successful, the thief goes off smiling.
  Surprised, that he carries the spoil.

A GIFT.

THE lovely Queen of Flowers
   One day a rose crown threw,
Each heart and petal, scented
   And crystal bright, with dew.
The very perfume smiling
   Like Orient's languid air,
Seemed tender as sweet reverié,
   Half veiled with twilight's prayer.

A little star of silver,
   More daring than the rest,
Crept softly in the Heaven's heart,
   The first to deck its crest.
A lonely bird uprising
   Sang in a forest deep,
A song, all soul enthrilling,
   Whilst earth was wrapped in sleep.

The moon, in vestal splendor,
   With virgin's holy grace
Rose slowly in her beauty,
   To tread her kingdom's space.
The sun had left a missive
   In golden letters fair,
And sealed it with a crimson kiss,
   Warm with a passion rare.

The day had flung her bridal veil,
   All silver fleece its hue.
And gleams of pearls and sapphire,
   Like spangles creeping through,

All nature, sun and breezes,
    Rare roses, fragrance sweet.
Birds, day and night-time splendor
    Flung incense at thy feet.

So, maiden, to their homage
    I, wealth to wealth impart,
But O, my gift outweighs them all;
    Mine is a human heart.

MY PRAYER.

[To my little niece, Bertha Marie.]

M Y little dove lies sleeping in her cradle,
    Her violet eyes soft closed, the while she dreams;
The angels must be breathing sweetest language,
    Such light upon my darling's face now gleams.
One tiny hand is clasping soft the other,
    And both uphold the sea shell-tinted face;
No artist ever could portray a picture
    Of such pure beauty, and unconscious grace.

But rarer far, my darling's priceless guerdon,
    The wealth that crowns her fair, sweet baby brow,
For such a monarch would resign his sceptre
    To but possess, what she is blessed with now.
Fair innocence, more grand than fame or glory—
    May never shadow rest on it to mar!
May it e'er stay as matchless in its beauty,
    As in the heavens remains some changeless star.

So as I kneel, and pray beside her cradle,
      Watching the while her dimples come, and go,
I think what shall I ask of God, to grant her;
      I scarce can answer, for I scarce can know.
I shall not ask that life be rainbow-tinted,
      Nor ceaseless sing joy's bonny, blithesome birds;
For such vain wishes, are but lightly spoken,
      Such hopes are naught, but shallow uttered words.

I will not ask that perfumed flowers will only
      Bloom brightly, without weeds, her path to strew,
I will not ask she be enframed in sunlight—
      It were not best thus—if I only knew—
I leave her little life, to One who's wiser;
      I only pray as now unstained she'll be,
When with her spotless wings from earth uplifted,
      My dove soars back into eternity.

A PICTURE.

A SUNSET sky, dyed with a rose heart's blush,
      A wealth of tropic palm,
A fountain plashing tamely in the midst,
      A death-like calm.

Two outstretched hands, a pleading, wistful face;
      Another turned away;
A tearless sob, wrung from a tortured heart,—
      Thus ends a day!

All nature, sun and breezes,
    Rare roses, fragrance sweet,
Birds, day and night-time splendor,
    Flung incense at thy feet.

A Gift. Page 63.   *Illustration by* EDWARD M. CAMPBELL.

LOVE AT PLAY.

L OVE held out his dimpled arms
     One fair morn whilst at his play,
To a maiden passing by,
     Pleading her with him to stay.
But she passed the laughing boy,
     Heeding not his roguish eye
Till upon her ear there fell
     Such a tender prayerful sigh.

Turning she beheld bright love,
     In the air above her rise.
All his laughter gone, instead
     Troubled depths within his eyes.
Then rose pity for his pain,
     Dreamed she not his wily ways
And she stood there, gentle soul,
     Listening as he eager prays.

Tarrying there in girlish grace
     Lo, the boy came nearer still.
And before her downcast eyes
     Could upraise, she felt a thrill
Wild and sweet, and strangely new.
     Winsome arms were round her cast,
And a rippling voice, low said
     "Now I have you, firm and fast."

Rare gleams lit his radiant orbs,
     And the brilliant rosy face
Bent, until the golden curls
     Kissed her brow's confiding grace.

Raised he then his rounded arms,
    Gentle seeming, yet how strong
And he tossed a jewelled chain,
    Singing soft this wooing song:

LOVE'S SONG.

"Come fair maid, be mine! be mine!
    I will throw this flashing chain,
'Twill link firm our throbbing hearts
    Till they ne'er can part again.

"I will lift thee 'mongst the stars,
    In their case of sapphire blue.
I will charge my golden friends,
    Shine still brighter for thy view.

"I will deck a couch for thee,
    Lined with scarlet poppies red
And their drowsy breaths shall woo
    Slumber to thy tired head.

"We will never touch the earth,
    Lest the dust should stain our feet,
Only mingle with the air
    Where the flowers have breathed it sweet!"

From his throat he swift unwound
    Garlands of bright crimson roses
All enwreathed by him who woos,
    On her head the crown reposes,
Flower-crowned and jeweled-chained,
    Smiles the maid beneath his kisses
And the winds that flash them by
    Tell the flowers of all their blisses.

Tho' the maid is lost to all
    Save the new and sweet caresses,
Never sees the stars above,
    Whilst his eye in love-light blesses,
Dimpled Love, all brightly smiling
    Often from her casts his eyes
Whispers to the passing winds,
    Flashes smiles upon the skies.

Suddenly midst perfumed air,
    Wings a gorgeous butterfly
Near him, and he longs to chase
    The bright creature, now so high.
"Ah, dear maid," he says, "farewell,
    Till I catch you beauty there,
Swift I shall return to thee,
    With the prize I'm sure to bear."

As she pleads him leave her not,
    He hath torn his arms away,
And her tear-filled eyes there see
    Night hath taken place of day.
Circling her the fetters still,
    But some links her feet lie under
And she sees herself firm chained
    Whilst Love's half is torn asunder.

Far on high the winged Love,
    While the gleaming butterfly
Leads her ardent follower on
    Farther, farther thro' the sky.
Farther, farther flash they on,
    Swiftly flying lost to sight,
Eager Love in mad pursuit
    Of his object of delight.

But ah, see when he has reached
    Close upon the rainbow wings
Suddenly a mist doth come
    And upon damp earth, Love flings.
With the creature he hath chased
    Vanished from before his eyes,
Sudden thoughts of her he'd left
    In his fickle bosom rise.

Flying once again to her
    All forgetting, months not days
Have on-sped, deep wonder comes
    At the sight that meets his gaze,
Summerland hath swept away.
    Autumn weather, wan and chill
Wraps all nature in her arms,
    Cloaks a maiden lying still.

Round her there, who prostrate lies
    Fetters chain the lily hands
Some have rusted from hot tears
    Some pure drops empearled the strands
Ah, the crimson roses hearts,
    And their petals all are dead.
Where the fragrant crown had been,
    Crumbling ashes wreathe her head.

On the cold dead form, doth Love
    Cast one sad repentant glance,
Till a weariness he feels,
    Rouses him from thoughtful trance.
"She was beautiful," he said,
    "And she still would fairer be!
How much pleasure I have lost,
    Foolish maid, to die for me!"

So the thoughtless boy then turned
Soon the ma d forgot at play,
Autumn was too chill for him,
On to Spring and radiant day !
From the Autumn, and the night
Swift the trifling boy had fled ;
But his flowers ashes, still
And his chairs, stay with the dead.

HEART RELICS.

ONLY a grave, in the depths of a heart,
Hidden away from the world's keen eyes;
Only a brook, with waves frozen o'er,
Masses .of clouds, where were blue summer skies.
Only a rose, that perished in bloom,
A bird that died, for a song it craved;
Only a melody, changed to a moan,
And a rag that once as a banner waved.

Only gray ashes, where flames burned bright,
A golden harp, with its strings all gone,
Only a dull stone, where a diamond flashed.
A wondrous star, grown pale and wan ;
Only a shadow, once roseate sun,
A bitter truth, once a dream of bliss ;
Only a sigh, out of dimpled smiles,
A cold chill breath, for a warm sweet kiss.

Only dark night, left of royal day,
A dream, once as sweet, as the violet's breath ;
Only dead leaves, out of verdure green,
A rose-like hope, that was touched by death.

These are all, yet she by them kneels,
  Bathed in the light of a past that glows,
Would she now rather they had never been?
  She cannot tell, ah, only God knows.

MURILLO'S IMMACULATE CONCEPTION.

FLOWING like a veil of sunlight
  Gleams her silken rippling hair
With her glorious eyes to heaven,
  Raised in mute and rapturous prayer
Features glowing soft in beauty,
  Every curve of grace so pure
Face of heavenly joy and patience
  Great to love, and to endure.

Like a lily, whose snow petals,
  Cannot hide the heart of gold,
On this lovely face the story
  Of her life is clearly told;
Gleams the purity of Heaven,
  Glows the strength of mother-love,
Deep the humble adoration
  Grand the glory from above.

Peace and hope, ecstatic gladness,
  Throw their light soft o'er her face;
Sweet, true prayers rise up within us,
  As we murmur, "Full of grace"
Could a human hand inspired
  Save by Heaven such beauty trace?
God reward thee great Murillo,
  For the gift of Mary's face.

THE LAST FAREWELL.

H OW can I bear it, love,
　　This parting! How to know
That never in the Winter winds,
　　Nor when the violets blow,
That never in the Autumn's chill,
　　Or warm bright Summer's breath,
Thy face may greet my eager sight?
　　Vain life in midst of death.

How can I bear it, darling,
　　Thou world of worlds to me!
When all the sun that ever shone
　　Sprang from my heart to thee?
Thy lightest tone, a sacred chime,
　　Thy soft caress Earth's grace
The lighthouse of tempestuous life
　　Thine earnest eyes and face.

My love, too pure for passion's reign,
　　'Tis love, and love alone,
And yet God help me that the strain
　　Hath sunk into a moan.
No more thy gentle clasp of hand,
　　No more to greet thine eyes;
Oh! exile, that I stand without
　　My gold-tinged Paradise.

We meet again in speechless pain,
　　We dare not frame one word,
For who would leap into a sea
　　By angry storm clouds stirred?

Nay, lest we seek the danger shoals
    We may not meet again,
We've battled with regret's strong force,
    Let not the war be vain.

But in this world my darling,
    My ideal realm, alone,
To-night I give my farewell kiss
    Most sacred in love's zone.
Oh! Let it holy fall, upon
    Thy phantom brow and lips,
How lurid burns the setting sun,
    Before the last eclipse!

The world hath lost its light to me,
    The song of life is done;
My royal crown I proudly wore,
    Is lost, ere scarce 'twas won.
But, oh! my darling, here to-night,
    In thought's deep pain and bliss,
I clasp you close within mine arms,
    To give my farewell kiss.
'Tis pure as thought of child at prayer,
    And so from wild regret,
Perhaps some day I yet may learn,
    To live and to—forget.

RETRIBUTION.

L OVE, the censer is lighted
　　To-night in my memory's shrine,
Dear, the incense is rising
　　In clouds, to this soul of mine,
Up from the swaying chalice
　　Comes the vapor of long dead dreams,
Up with the clouds of incense
　　Comes the perfume of love-lit gleams.

Oh ! but the mists are diffusing
　　My heart with a drear regret,
Oh ! but the perfume is proving
　　My soul that it cannot forget.
Oh ! they undo in their wreathings
　　The lessons I've schooled by heart,
Oh ! they burn in pain in my bosom
　　With the spectres their mists impart.

Oh ! the censer that sways a-lighted
　　Grows dim with the damp of tears
And the incense grows black from its violet
　　By the storms of a thousand fears,
Dear, your face is before me,
　　That face that must always gleam,
Uplooking, as sad and mournful
　　As the ghost of my own dead dream.

Can it be that memory will soften
　　Some day till it melt away,
So far, that I'll lose the vision
　　Which darkeneth every day ?

No, whilst there is memory left me
    Its fairies must ring the knell,
And toll of the solemn funeral
    Of one whom I loved too well.

Of one in my heart's lone grave yard,
    Who, pulsing in happy youth
In life, with mortals, is breathing,
    Lies dead on the bier of Truth,
Dead e'en tho' the lips be scarlet, .
    Dead e'en though the heart beats high,
Dead, e'en though the voice is ringing
    In jest as it passeth me by.

Dead, e'n though my heart is breaking,
    That the beautiful form's uncold,
And the red lips not faded forever,
    That smile now so scornfully bold.
Dear, it were better, aye better,
    When we buried our love one day,
That we in the earthland, together
    Were silently hidden away.

Ah! smile, but you feel as anguished
    As I, in your soul to-night,
Go, laugh in the world's gay glamor!
    But you dare not before God's sight.
You may jeer at your own emotions,
    Scoff too, at the times now gone,
But your heart is as pale, and mournful
    Your soul is as chill and wan

As the mist of a bleak October
    Which follows the summer's sun,

And sighs that it still must linger
  When the light of its life is done.
Dear, others who saw not the beauty
  Of the soul, that I knew so well,
Dream not of the pain and passion
  In the heart where regret must dwell.

Love swayeth the censer slowly,
  Oh! God, if Thou would'st but will
That the heart and the censer it holdeth
  Lay calm in the awful still!

——— — ———

LOUISE.

A ND oh, the sun was gleaming bright
  Above the sweet fields, that day,
And I thought a maiden, from out his court
  Was coming to cross my way.
I saw her tripping, the winsome lass,
  Like a fawn to where stood I,
And the warmth from the Heavens, stole softly down
  And bathed her in golden dye.

O'er her gypsy face, there was lightly placed,
  A crownlet of flowers gay,
And daisies, and poppies caressed her hair
  Which blew with the breath of May.
A thousand times I can see those eyes,
  A-glowing with light and love ;
With all the ardor of poppies rare,
  Yet pure as the white winged dove.

She seemed a creature of morn and day—
  Not one of the stars, and night,
And my heart leaped up with affection's throb
  At the beautiful vision bright.
God grant, prayed I, that the sunlight cling
  And burnish the pure young soul;
God grant, prayed I, that the ardent mind
  May climb to the longed-for goal.

A vision of roses, spring and love
  Is my dark-eyed gypsy queen,
And truly no sweeter picture could
  In life of a mortal be seen.
Bright fairies are ringing a golden chime
  About the form of the vision there,
But the angels above, guard soft the soul
  And flood it ever with faith and prayer.

THE DIFFERENCE.

WHY do you ask for a word from me, dearest,
  When the least, uttered, were better unsaid?
Why do you ask for a brief Resurrection,
  Of the dear love, that were better now dead?
Why do you taunt me, with wholly forgetting?
  Why do you challenge me, just for one word?
Heaven was pitiful—can you regret it,
  And call up the pain, that 'twere mercy unstirred?

Why do you boast of your faithful remembrance?
  Know you not roses are sweet but in bloom?
Why do you seek for the pale withered petals,
  That shake in the drear winds which shriek round a tomb?
I have forgotten, you say, oh, just Heaven!
  Can you know, then, what I've suffered to gain
· Just the calm surface, to smile as I bear it:
  To know that our love was a dream all in vain?

"*I* have forgotten," and *you* "have remembered,"
  Yet did you kneel, as for months long I did;
Yet did you writhe in the throes of soul torture
  And close with your own hand your heart's coffin lid.
Oh, no, you taunt, for you felt not as I do,
  Duty is just—as the Fates willed, you thought,
And now that I conquered, and crushed down rebellion,
  You'd fain to a new life, Love's passion be brought.

No, not a word, not a little line, dearest,
  Nay, not a thought in the old pulsing way.
Months, did I watch in despair by my dying,
  Perhaps my heart broke, on the last fatal day.

With my weak hands did I stifle, and crush it,
    With my white hands, did I put it away,
There shall it rest, 'neath the pall of oblivion.
    There shall the ghost of a pale passion lay.

Challenge me! Taunt me! And scorn, if you will, then,
    But ask not a rose, where the roses are dead.
And ask not a song from a bird that's now voiceless,
    From whose golden throat all the music hath fled,
"Still, do I love you?" Oh cruellest question,
    Stars high above as you gleam in the skies,
You who have seen us together can answer,
    You who have seen that light, once in my eyes.

You also have looked, as he kissed me that evening,
    Waking my soul to a new pulsing birth,
Burning my heart, with the heat of his passion,
    Lifting me, drifting my soul from this earth.
You who have seen me clasped close, in caresses,
    Watched his dear eyes as they challenged mine own,
Heard his soft whispers, and heard my replying,
    Tell him, oh, stars, Love is deathless alone.
But to you, dearest, not one word or whisper;
    Surely such answer were better unsaid.
Surely no ghosts of unrest, and wild longing,
    Should mar the calm peace, that now shrineth my dead.

AN AWAKENING.

IT was just a careless cresting,
   Of a stranger's head to-day,
That swept me from the present
   To the dear lost far away,
I thought I had forgotten,
   That the dream of early youth
Lay too chilled for resurrection
   On the bier of perfect truth.

I had thought your face forever
   Could wake no throb for me,
That the memory, like the passion
   Dead, had drifted from life's sea,
But just the careless cresting
   Of a stranger's head, to-day,
Brought back to pulsing anguish
   All I thought was swept away.

I had thought, in hopeful trusting
   You, once my king 'mongst men
Were forgotten, for my darling
   I have suffered so since then,
But to-night I crept to dreamland,
   And from the world of care,
I drew the key of long ago
   And shut out dull despair.

And there alone in dreamland,
   I knelt, by Fate's deep sea
And eager clasped the sea shells
   To sing their songs to me.

I held them fraught with music
    So closely to my ear
They whispered—little traitors—
    And told me you were near.

They sang soft of one rare dream
    When we loved, dear, you and I!
When I to you was all the world,
    And, you my stars, and sky,
I thrilled with love, not passion
    For a first love's, love alone,
I since have felt the rapture
    When warm passion mounts her throne.

For passion's, smiles and roses
    Moonlight and starry air,
But a first love's when the Angels
    Smile on us midst their prayer.
Oh, silent grew the sea shells,
    The songs were swiftly o'er
Upon the stage the curtain
    Of the past swept down once more.

But it taught me, this, the cresting
    Of the stranger's head to-day,
That little movement, so like yours
    In the dear far away,
That out of passion, pain and strife,
    However chilled life be,
The love that crowned us first, awakes
    The heart's eternity.

Let memory like
The song of Love,
Drive away tear
which sorrow brings
Back to the heart
From which it springs,
And make such flowers
With fragrance rare,
To bloom from year
To year

Singing soft this wooing song:

LOVE'S SONG.

"Come fair maid, be mine! be mine!
*   *   *   *   *

"I will deck a couch for thee,
  Lined with scarlet poppies red
And their drowsy breaths shall woo
  Slumber to thy tired head."

THE PARTING.

TAKE it, dear love, the blood-red rose I send.
　　Deep, deep within its heart there lies my kiss.
Take it, and press it to your lips, and say
　　"Renunciation crowns the ghost of bliss."
　　　　This is the end.

When crushed in trembling fragrance, on your mouth,
　　Across the warm sweet meeting, let no chill
Creep in the sacrifice that spans our love,
　　Whisper with me, "'Tis best, for 'tis His will,
　　　　That it must end."

Let then the death-cup, that must still our love,
　　Be sweet to you, brought in the heart of rose.
It suits you best, but I—I shall kneel down
　　Where bleak and crear, and deep it snows,
　　　　To watch the end.

Out, out where cold winds sweep my colder soul,
　　And knife-edged blasts cut keenly in my heart,
Where shines no star, above the sullen clouds,
　　There shall I watch, alone, our love depart
　　　　Chilled at the end.

Roses, and sunlight be the death-cup, dear,
　　To drown your love for me, 'tis better so.
To you, accustomed to the warmth and wine
　　But mine shall be the chilling cup of snow,
　　　　To bring the end.

HER STORY—AND MINE.

UNDER the gas light musing—
    Just as he left her there,
With one cream rose soft nestling
    In the wealth of her gold-brown hair
And a cluster of rainbow flowers
    In fern on her bosom laid,
That rose with the quickened breathing
    The throbbing girl-heart made.

Under the gas light musing—
    With a smile on her sweet pure face
And a glorious light enwreathing
    Her form from its proud young grace,
With her beautiful eyes unknowing
    Transfixed on the flowers fair,
Which smile in a silent fragrance
    Sweet stars in Love's perfumed air.

And the story she's just been learning,
    Illumined with joy from above,
That has come to bless her soul-life,
    In the form of a snow-white dove.
Under the gas light musing—
    In laces and robes of cream,
With her luminous eyes of sapphire,
    A match for her diamonds gleam.

And a rose, and its leaf has fallen,
    Half trampled beneath her feet,
Yet she stands in her stately beauty
    A queen with her crown complete.

And the charming lips are parted
　　With a smile of wonderful grace,
Whilst the gleaming pearls are gemming
　　The depths of their coral case.

Under the gas light musing—
　　Just as he left her there,
With her heart sweet filled with fragrance
　　By the rose he had planted there.
And the hours swept by unnoted,
　　Till the tiny clock of gold,
Just utters a sign of warning
　　That the last hour of day is told.

　　　*　　*　　*　　*　　*　　*　　*

Under the moonlight silent—
　　Just as he left her there,
With one heliotrope soft clinging
　　In the wealth of gold-brown hair,
And the same sweet purple flowers,
　　All drooped on her bosom fair
The blossoms swaying so softly
　　They echo no throbbing there.

Under the moonlight silent—
　　With the beautiful head drooped low,
And one small white hand clutching
　　Her dress, though she does not know,
With the lovely face so pallid,
　　And the lips so pained and white,
With the glorious eyes of sapphire,
　　All robbed of their radiant light.

Under the moonlight silent —
　　Like a flower so crushed and wan,
When the joy of the sun, and dew drops
　　From its heart is forever gone.
Under the moonlight silent —
　　Just as he left her there,
Then she learned the story of losing
　　Out in the night-time air.

Then she learned of the world's false glamor,
　　And the dead sea fruit, called love,
Then she raised her eyes all tearless,
　　To the Only Truth, above.
She stands in her girlish beauty,
　　A queen in her woman's pride
Yet a wounded child in sorrow,
　　That the night-clouds cannot hide.

Under the moonlight silent —
　　Just as he left her there,
With the heliotropes swift dying,
　　Like her dream, in the night-time air
With the icy sternness of winter
　　In her heart, on her face, despair
Or a vague half doubting wonder,
　　Just as he left her there.

*   *   *   *   *   *   *

Under the taper light burning —
　　Marble-cold and fair,
With one lily chalice resting
　　In the midst of the gold-brown hair.

And a cluster upon her bosom
    All cold on the statue breast,
Under the taper light lying
    Asleep in the awful rest.

Under the taper light lying—
    Under the solemn light,
She lay like a pallid star gleam
    Asleep on the breast of night.
Dark lashes sweeping the waxen
    Of the beautiful cold dead face,
Under the taper light lying
    Like a dream, in a dream of grace.

With the light of the eyes all darkened,
    With the brow 'neath Death's icy crown,
With the small pale hands crossed softly,
    But the hair, just the same gold brown.
Under the taper light lying—
    I watch the still white form,
With the mantle of Death around it,
    Yet clothed with imperial charm.

And I saw him stand above her
    She lying so calmly there,
And I saw him stoop and softly
    Caress the gold-brown hair,
And I saw him sad and solemn,
    Great tears in his handsome eyes,
But knew they were only passing
    Swift clouds on his careless skies.

And I hated him as he stood there
    With his careless handsome face,

For I knew he had laid my darling
　　There low in her sable case,
And I hated him, for I knew how
　　Were life in that beautiful form,
The heart would quicken, and robe him
　　Once more in the old-time charm.

If she felt his eyes were upon her,
　　Warm, soft as I saw them now,
How her sorrowed soul would forgive him,
　　His passionate, faithless vow.
Under the taper light lying—
　　Beautiful, pallid, and cold,
And only two of the watchers
　　Dreamed why her life was told.

Yea, tears in his eyes, I saw them
　　As he looked on the cold dead face,
Tears, fickle tears of the moment,
　　One hour alone would efface.

All thoughts of the one who loved him,
　　As only a woman can, who
Loves with deepest passion of mortal
　　Whilst keeping dear Heaven in view,
Oh! had he but come to her living,
　　Caressing the silken hair,
Not under the taper light lying—
　　Would my darling be sleeping there.

Yet pure, with the glow of Heaven,
　　'Thwart her face like a holy gleam,
I knew it were better she rested
　　Asleep with her own dead dream.

Under the taper light lying—
    He turned and he left her there,
With the vestal lilies crowning
    Her breast, and her gold-brown hair.

Turning, he softly left her,
    Warm tears in his handsome eyes,
But I stood there chill, and tearless,
    As the cloud of December skies,
Coldly I stood by my darling,
    Who never gave thought to me,
With my passionate heart wild crying
    For the bitter never to be.

Yea, softly he passed and vanished,
    Just heaving a careless sigh,
But I staid, till they all had left her,
    All—save the lilies and I.

————

A DEVOTEE.

[In a Gainsborough Hat.]

AND, oh, she was lovely!
    And, oh, she was fair!
With the sungleams caressing
    The brown of her hair ;
With royal sweet lovelights
    Enthroned in her eyes,
Dark-lashed, in their sapphire
    As deep as the skies.

With mouth sweet and riante,
Yet, tender withal,
And face like a snowdrift
Where sun-kisses fall.
And, oh, she was lovely,
And, oh, she was fair,
With a Gainsborough hat,
And its plumes on her hair.

'Twas framing a picture
Of beauty and grace,
And crowning a poem
An angel might trace.
And, oh, she was modest,
And gentle and rare.
For I watched her in church
As she knelt bowed in prayer.

And never I saw her
Again, but afar
In my life seems there fallen
A sweet holy star.
Oft rises the vision
I saw at her prayer,
With a Gainsborough hat
And its plumes on her hair.

THE FADED VALENTINE.

M Y lady sits in her boudoir fair,
  In the firelight, and perfumed air,
There are painted china, and bronzes bright,
There are lamps that glow, with an amber light,
Rare bric-a-brac, and sculpture's gleam.
She seems the heart of this glowing dream,
There in her gown of cream brocade,
With a mist of lacé, on her brown hair laid.

And the slippered feet, tap up and down
From their hiding place, 'neath the cream tea-gown.
'Tis a jeweled nest, for the bright-plumed bird,
Then why is my lady so strangely stirred?
There with her beautiful head at rest
On one slim hand, with the diamond's crest,
That catches the firelight's flash and glow —
Why is it my lady is musing so?

Without, are snowflakes in the air,
And she languidly watches them falling there,
As her deep, low chair tilts to and fro,
In the softened warmth of the firelight's glow.
But now there arises a swift sweet gleam
In her wine-dark eyes, like a new born dream,
And, musing awhile, my lady turns,
And the firelight glows, and the firelight burns.

And the bric-a-brac, and the amber rare
Sparkle, and flash in the rose-filled air.
She rises and draws from a cabinet
A faded spray of mignonette,

And a paper yellow, and faded too,
And tied with a ribbon of sapphire hue,
And airy Cupids and roses bright
Look strangely sad on the paper's blight.

But ah, they're not faded for her I trow,
For my lady is kneeling with troubled brow,
And tears are falling on Cupid's face,
And tears are dimming the faint ink trace,
And tears are flecking the mignonette —
(And yet they tell us that hearts forget —)
And so in the boudoir, dainty, fair,
My lady weeps in her heart's despair

And the amber lights of the lamps that shine
May not brighten her valentine.
Old, and faded and dim with years —
Oh, there's reason enough for a storm of tears.
But steps are coming, she hears their fall,
And she rises to answer her husband's call,
And hastily hides the mignonette,
And the Cupids' faces with tears still wet.

And so in the firelight's flash and glow
We can guess why my lady was musing so,
For memory troops with her shining array
And many a heart sobs on Valentine's Day.

ROMOLA — SELF EXILED.

SHE rose and sadly left Love's 'chanted land,
  But one deep, searching gaze a-backward turned,
Then onward with her pallid face of woe,
  And eyes in which the fire of anguish burned.
But ever and anon, she paused and stood,
  Compelled to seek with eyes the fading land;
And ever and anon grief's burning crept
  Into her face, new-born resolve made grand.

She saw the once great place, where only now
  A mocking ghost rose up, within the throne;
She saw the air with fleeing spirits filled,
  The phantoms followed laughing Love alone;
She saw a lovely ship on Truth's clear lake
  Sail down the waves, and vanish into mist;
She saw a figure, Trust, in violet robes,
  Stand there alone, sole keeper of a tryst.

She saw two goblets of a shadowy gold
  Stand emptied of their draughts of flashing wine;
She saw the birds, all drooping and unvoiced,
  The dewdrops once, now crystalized to brine;
She saw the flowers change to ashes gray,
  And two sweet harps, devoid of glittering strings;
She saw the fountains, once so plashing bright,
  Rush dreary by o'er dark and rocky springs.

And whiter grew her face, more shuddering seemed
  Her form whilst pathos of a heart's despair
Gathered to cloud her pathway like to night,
  And stifling make the new-found cheerless air,

She onward sped, till with a last resolve,
　　Stood calm, and, gazing with hot, tearless eyes.
Swept back her glance, as lovely Eve once did,
　　When fleeing from her radiant Paradise.

Lo! with a clash the gates of Love's land closed,
　　And falling on her knees, she bitter moaned:
"Mocked! mocked by Love! Whose Queen so late I reigned;
　　Now, exiled, I, all crownless and dethroned,
And he my former King, lies low in dust,
　　A fallen god, who charmed with golden glow,
Who but deceived my eyes, won my deep heart
　　With arts, which treacherous Fancy loves to throw."

"Mocked! mocked!" she cried, "My joy and youth all gone,
　　Exiled, I wander from Love's sunny land;
But lo!" uplifting proud her dusky eyes,
　　"Is there no goal less beautiful, more grand,
Is there no goal whose silver stars point out
　　True aspirations, from each self apart,
Whose hopes, and aims lead to holier things
　　Than housing only each a selfish heart."

"Farewell, dear land, the mist is deepening o'er
　　Your space. I go, farewell, all self-exiled,
But not to seek the river dark Despair,
　　Rather to find a haven undefiled."
Uprose she then in queenly majesty,
　　And on her crownless head she clasped her hands,
Poor, trembling hands! But passed she stately on,
　　Heavy, but brave, to seek those other lands.
And travelers treading the same dreary road,
　　A woman saw, in silent, holy guise,
In whose calm face Peace symbolized itself,
　　But wore a twilight in the dusky eyes.

A LIFE COMPLETE.

IN MEMORY CF MRS. ELIZA McKEE.

SILENT the harp, life's music chilled and hushed,
    Where once flowed melody like holiest dream,
And yet the echo always will be here
    To soothe with memory's softly chastened gleam.

For in her hands the harp a symbol was
    Of God's rare music where each soft-touched chord
Breathed mercy, charity and peaceful love,
    And soothing balm to life's keen, hurtful sword.

And as she passed upon her stately way,
    Dropping a pearl with each sweet outstretched hand
To those less fortunate, less blest than she
    Life's harp proclaimed the music sweet and grand.

Time winged its flight, youth's springtime violets died,
    · And roses came in summer's richer sway,
And then the tinted leaves of autumn trees,
    And after winter's snows, with frost tinged day.

Lo! the chill touched! The generous hand was stilled,
    And pulseless that brave heart within the breast,
That never beat save with impulses grand,
    That sought and wcn the Christian's right of rest.

And by her side the silent harp lay still,
    The golden chords mute for the hand to string
Their melody in praise of Him she loved,
    Of Him she knew from whom all blessings spring.

Violets and roses, leaves and winter's snow
    All left their tribute in her life complete,
Till as she closed her eyes and clasped her hands
    Across her heart there lay the golden wheat.

A life complete. A story grandly told,
    A song that came from God's own will, to cheer,
These were the lights that decked the silent form,
    And formed the tapers clustered o'er her bier.

But for the silent one, ah, who would weep?
    'Twere not for tears to fall on bright renown,
And who with eyes upon the restful face
    But knew her head already wore the crown.

And in the hearts of those who knew her well
    Each held the rosary of her good deeds done,
And stopped the human tears, for who dare weep
    For heaven's sceptre bravely sought and won?

And o'er her memory pearls of love are laid,
    Trust sways her censer with its incense sweet,
And over all there lies in stateliness,
    The palm of all, the sheaf of golden wheat.

No tears for her, but for that other heart,
    The one so dear, whose gentle life was twined,
Like roses in the laurel of her love,
    Ah, sorrow in her sable is enshrined.

And grief throbs warm, for who may know the void,
    The tender love that's missed each passing day,
The word, the smile, the loving, soft caress?
    She feels a starless night where once was day.

For her the cross, for her that awful space,
  That voiceless loss, that ever sad refrain,
Where longing droops her over-burdened heart,
  As echo whispers " ne'er in life again."

Not e'er in life, but, with brave eyes upraised
  To where the crucifix has taught her trust,
There comes the soothing hope of that some-day,
  When endless meeting rises from life's dust.

And once again the hearts that loved in life
  Meet dearer for the suffering parting gave,
And she shall know re-union in the life,
  The only life, the one beyond the grave.

THE DEATH OF LOVE.

OUT, the wind sighing; in, Love is dying,
  Breathing his last in despair,
Whilst I am kneeling, in sad appealing,
  Down by the dear form in prayer.
Oh! he is going, life is fast flowing,
  Bearing Love on to his death;
Out, the wind roaring; in, I imploring
  Kisses, whilst yet he hath breath.

Ah, but he's flown! only air blown
  Chill, strikes my heart from without;
In shroud that I fear, Love lies on his bier,
  Slain by keen arrows of doubt,
Hushed I will lay him, (I did not slay him)
  Soft in the grave he has won,
Out, the wind sighing; in, I am crying,
  Trust, thou forever art done.

A THOUGHT.

OUT of clouds of soul-life, darling,
    Gleam your darkly earnest eyes,
Ever glowing, ever liquid
    In their depths like sun-warm skies.
Not gay Fancy's bright battalion,
    Laughing nymphs, and naiads fair
Tease my thoughts to weave this rainbow
    Interspersed with rose-kissed air.

Not ambitious love of lustre
    Encores Fame to play again,
Deep to steep the mind in incense,
    Subtly tingling every vein.
Not cold Friendship lights her tapers
    With their pale, dull amber glare,
Nor the filmy frost-veil, longing,
    Wafts me to enchanted air.

Not Affection's stars half silver,
    Showing oft a hint of gold,
Nor Reflection's shadowy moonbeams
    Shafts of pallid thought unrolled.
No, 'tis Love lights Memory's fires,
    Feeding them with hallowed coals,
Blinding, burning, till they'd scorch me
    With their rose deep glowing souls.

Save that o'er the pyre thus standing
    Ever near in splendid mien
One sweet form that's urging onward
    Like some grand, brave-hearted queen;

Old, and faded and dim with years—
Oh, there's reason enough for a storm of tears.
   *   *   *   *   *   *   *   *

And so in the firelight's flash and glow
We can guess why my lady was musing so.

A Faded Valentine. Page 90.   *Illustration by* PAUL E. HARNEY.

And ah, clear those darkly earnest
    Eyes are gleaming through Thought's haze,
All to-night to fill my dreamings
    With their soul-illumined rays

Circles of a thousand pleasures,
    Flash their iridescent hues,
All unnoted shine their treasures,
    Thrice unwelcome as I muse.
No, the shadow of one love-time
    Following too ardent sun,
And the elfin sprites of sorrow,
    Whisper of a time that's done.

Whisper of some once rare kisses
    Rose hearts blended into one,
Whisper of some soft caresses,
    Each a world too swiftly spun ;
Whisper of those low-toned voicings,
    Love-words each of silver spray,
Whisper of symbolic starlight
    Sweeter than the glaring day.

Ever beautiful and cherished
    Eyes that cleave my very soul,
We can scorn the life that parts us,
    Once we reached Love's highest goal ;
I will ask the dear sweet angels
    To bear words to-night, to thee,
All unknowing, we together
    In blest Memory's aisle shall be.

MY LADY'S MOOD.

MY Lady in her willow chair,
    Is tilting to and fro,
Upon her fair, proud face the tint
    Of rose-lights softly glow.
Within the slumbrous depths of rare
    Wine-golden eyes, a gleam,
My Lady in a waking trance
    Is lost within a dream
Her little hand, half carelessly
    Toys with her amber hair,
Or rests unconscious in its sweep,
    Upon the white breast — bare.
Her proud, sweet face is captive now;
    In musing's reign, is tossed.
And in the tempest retrospect,
    Her pondering soul is lost.

My Lady in her golden nest
    Is throned the jewel there,
And diamonds star her pulsing throat
    And nestle in her hair,
Upon her proudly classic head,
    Is Luxury's diadem cast,
But, oh! within the smiling eyes
    There lurks a shadowed past.

Smiles deck her now with crystal gleams
    Pearls mark patrician sway,
But, oh! to reach the limpid waves
    What breakers on the way,
Sighs darkened every hopeful light,
    Sobs wrung her soul in twain,

And all was storms and hot unrest,
    No dew drops lulled the pain.
Her pride knelt in its widowed garb,
    Her heart wept in her breast,
Self, crouching still, she waged the war
    And wears to-day a — crest.

She battled as no soldier could,
    She hewed the boulders down,
She loosed the ice with scalding tears
    And wore the thorns a crown.
She even lifted high her eyes
    To God in Heaven, for aid
And with the sceptre of her soul
    The cruel foe she stayed.

Ah! me, My Lady's musing there,
    The rose-lamp's burning bright,
What cares she for the snow-filled air,
    Without the sombre night?
Yet dreaming she, in willow chair,
    Sits tilting too and fro,
The fire light upon her face,
    Within her eyes its glow.

My Lady in her fleecy robes,
    Is strangely pale and still,
Within her rainbow-jewelled nest
    There creeps a vague weird chill
For, can bright jewels quiet pain,
    Or lights, heal wounded pride?
My Lady were the happier
    If she a child, had died!

THE OLD AND THE NEW.

" Le Roi est mort, vive le Roi ! "

THE OLD.

AH, he died softly, soft as a tear,
   Low with his sceptre, laid on his bier.
Leave him the crown that encircles his head,
Let it still cling to the poor frozen dead.
Fold those white hands o'er the wide quiet breast,
Ceaseless in life, oh, disturb not their rest.
Throw round his form as 'tis laid deep away,
Strings of pearl memories ever to stay.

Place the dry flowers, once rose-colored dreams,
Bury them with him, now past are their gleams;
Sing a sad dirge o'er the form lying cold,
This last holy favor, oh, do not withhold.
Cry not aloud of his faults, or his sins,
Time hath demanded the debt, folly wins.
Dwell on the good that his sceptre did wield,
Pray that the seeds shall beflower life's field.

Love him, if but for the silvered-o'er hair,
Pity him deep, for the traces of care ;
Ring, gentle bells, o'er his funeral bier,
This be your grief for the stricken Old Year.

THE NEW.

All hail! oh, Boy Sovereign! Ring, chimes gaily now!
As proudly he stands, his new crown on his brow;
Bright roses are wreathing his beautiful form,
Breathing their perfume like incense so warm ;

O'er him a banner is proudly unfurled,
Monarch he stands on his footstool, the World.
Greet him with music; high, high let it swell,
Ring o'er his head Mirth's clear, chiming bell.

Sprinkle bright holly, to deck with its red
Each passing step that the youthful feet tread.
Ah, let each soul greet him gayly to-night,
Pray that his reign be a mantle of Right;
Vow that you serve him with honor most dear—
This be your greeting unto the New Year.

ALPHA—OMEGA.

A TINY germ, beneath the moist earth laid,
But lo! one day a golden sunlight came
And drew it from the ground, into the world,
And brought it into loveliness and fame.
And so it burst, a blossom beautiful
All bathed its face and heart in crystal dew,
And wreathed with golden shafts from out the sun
And fanned by zephyrs as they onward flew;
            And this was life!

One day a flower bloomed, all stately fair
Within a garden, and the sun-king swept
His harp to tune her beauty, and the dew
Laughed that its silver sweetly crept her through.
But lo! a cloud swift massed above the spot;
An ebon gloom dark as the midnight's breast
And crashed into a storm. The flower swayed,
Scattering in atoms, as the cold winds pressed;
            And this was death!

FRUITLESS.

WEEP not o'er him, silent sleeping
    In his bed beneath the snow!
Sob not, as the wind's harsh wailings
    O'er that lonely spot now go!
Hush, his life was like their moanings,
    Chilled sometimes, then hot, and wild,
And no sun shed gleams of brightness,
    No sweet skies above him smiled.

Do not deck his grave with roses;
    He who never felt their charm;
What availeth now their perfume
    To that cold and lifeless form?
What availeth their bright color
    To those dark and rayless eyes?
Does the stricken bird e'er warble
    To the sapphire of the skies?

If in life you had but given
    One small flower of hope, and love;
All its sprays would bright have blossomed
    In God's home for you above.
If by tear of warning, pity,
    Or a smile of cheerful ray,
You had helped his tired footsteps
    On his thorn-pierced, weary way,

But you left him toiling, wounded,
    Battling, blind with burning tears;
Disappointment's robe enwrapt him,
    Doubt assailed with all her fears.

You, who sped upon your pathway,
    Smiling bright as spring-time air,
Gave no generous hand to aid him,
    No soft word to help him bear.

Cease your wailings! Tears are fruitless,
    If not false. Too late they fall.
Leave him to his lonely sleeping,
    Sob not, o'er his funeral pall!
Take your flowers, they are mocking;
    Did he have one lifetime rose?
God, who knew him, loved him, pitied,
    Raised his soul from earthly woes,

THINE EYES.

THY gentle eyes, my darling,
    They haunt me with their gleams,
So limpid sweet and saddened,
    Like ghost of happy dreams.
Within their liquid amber,
    In the depths of their chaste light,
I can read a broad heart history,
    And I feel I read it right.

'Neath the veil of resignation,
    'Neath the courage monarch there
Creeps the shadow of heart-weeping,
    Gleams the echo of a prayer.
Soft the lights, and lustrous, darling,
    Yet the lustre's chastened glow,
Seems like stars that smile in triumph
    At a meeting with the snow.

Saw you, darling, in the zenith
    Of the tranquil last night-time,
The fair moon, that sailed above us
    With a beauty grand, sublime ?
Saw you 'neath its regal splendor,
    That its pure and tender glow
Told it knew of brightest blisses,
    But alas, far more of woe ?

So it seems, my gentle darling,
    Glow your amber eyes to me.
They are starlights of existence,
    With the queen moon's memory.
Ah, they haunt me in the stillness,
    With their saddened, tender gleams ;
For they seem a book of histories,
    And reflect a host of dreams.

Ah, no poet, deep, impassioned,
    Could a poem rare unfurl,
Like the soft poetic, vision
    That those liquid depths impearl.
Ah, no artist's brush inspired,
    Could portray a picture fair
As those tender orbs are framing,
    Like some grand, imploring prayer.

Oh, they haunt me with their gleaming,
    With their freight of by-gone years.
For within their sad, calm smiling,
    Do I note their sea of tears.

LOVE'S ROSE.

" DO I love him?" asked the maiden,
  With her pretty face all dyed
By the gentle roseate blushes
  Which the lilies could not hide—
Idly pulls she there the petals
  Of a full-blown crimson rose;
And, retaining heart all golden,
  To the wind each petal throws.

Soft she whispers, "Oh, my darling.
  I do love thee fond and dear;
Sweetheart, every tone is precious,
  I, but live when thou art near.
Will I be thine own, my darling
  Oh! I dare not be thy bride,
For I have a stronger passion
  Than my love; men call it pride.

"Could he foster my ambition,
  Let me rule, a very queen,
Clothe my form in costly raiment,
  Deck me with the diamond's sheen?
I am beautiful, they tell me,
  And I must have royal power;
Love, it cannot last forever,
  It is but a rapturous hour.

"Yet my love is oh, so gentle!
  And the smiles that light his eyes
Make me feel when I am near him
  That I dwell in Paradise.

Still I yearn for glittering glory,
    I am vassal to my pride;
Yes, I love my darling fondly,
    But I may not be his bride.''

So she plucked the rose half idly,
    With the only petal left
Tossed afar the heart all golden,
    And of flowers stood bereft.

      o   o   o   o   *

After years she stands a woman;
    Sweeping robes of satin-sheen
Fitly frame the splendid picture
    Of this careless, haughty queen.
Proudly curve the lips of carmine,
    Glows the lustre of the eyes.
Shining dusky as two storm-clouds
    That have crossed blue summer skies.

Diamonds flash like brilliant meteors,
    Sparkle with their witch-like glow,
Poppies deck the scornful bosom,
    And their languor o'er her throw.
But amid that pomp and splendor
    She would give her life, to-day
To live over but that hour
    When she threw her rose away.

A RAINY DAY.

TEARS are falling moist and gentle
    From the great heart of the sky,
Dropping like a grief, though human,
    Tender from the Heaven nigh,
Nature, like a woman sobbing,
    Weeps out all her care and pain;
Weeps that in the birth of many
    Years, she's suffered but in vain.
Suffered that her new-born children
    Spring, alas! to days of care;
Suffered, that she gives existence
    Where the birth but brings despair.

Ah! She sees, this watchful mother,
    Every dull, and hidden strife,
Grieves o'er all the heat and struggle,
    Pride and tumult of this life.
Where some bright new son outspringing,
    Waves his cap, and plunges far
In the world's warfare and battle;
    Like a brilliant, changeful star
Flashes in the world's arena,
    Climbs, and conquering wins the game.
Then, rewarding all his valor,
    Smiles proud nature o'er his fame.

When some brilliant, laughing daughter
    Trips out gaily on life's stage,
Queenly growing, from free homage
    Makes the fickle world her page.

When their Father Time throws baubles
    O'er her babes, who laugh the while,
Then it is, pleased Mother Nature
    Shows the sunshine of her smile.

But ah! deeper, holier loves she
    Those poor children who are born
Slow of intellect, or purpose,
    Or of happy fortune shorn.
Those poor babes who slowly travel
    Weakened by the constant fight,
Those, her children, who half sinking
    Yet still, bravely front the fight.
And, oh! for those helpless lost ones
    Who too weak, have fallen low.
Over these the shame-faced mother
    Weeps in all her mighty woe.

Days of sunshine are her smilings,
    Days of rain, her heart is filled
Till o'erflowing from its burden,
    Down on earth, the tears are spilled.
Smiles, and tear drops, form her heart-life,
    Laughs, and sighs become the world
Over all the wondrous wisdom
    Of God's will, is wide unfurled.
So, in gloom, the day is weeping
    Just to ease her watchful heart.
Clouds, and sun, and light and shadows,
    Are the sum of Nature's part.

HOW COME THE STARS?

THE ASTRONOMY OF LITTLE CONSTANCE.

SHE was a lovely gentle child,
  Her face a lily fair,
A golden wealth enwreathing it,
  Her eyes, two books of prayer,

We sat together, this fair eve
  In quiet, she and I,
Our eyes were fixed upon the stars
  That flowered all the sky.
One little hand was clasped in mine,
  Her head drooped on my breast,
My hand half idly sweeping through
  The shining silken crest.

Those blue forget-me-nots her eyes
  She raised, and softly said —
Her voice, you know, was like a harp
  Just to the night winds wed.
So gentle that it held a scroll
  Of songs in every tone,
Sometimes I closed my eyes and thought
  'Twas Angel's voice alone ;

But then she spoke as there we sat
  Together, she and I,
For I half carelessly, had asked
  Her version of the sky,

And said: "My darling, tell me what
  Makes all those stars above,
Those golden stars, those gentle stars,
  That you and I so love?"

Then answered she, "Why don't you know
  The sky is Heaven's own floor,
The angels kneel there all about
  When dear God they adore,
And when the clouds go sweeping by
  They leave each, many a space;
And then the light of Heaven shines through
  Right down upon Earth's face.

And to our eyes, God's floor's the sky,
  And to our eyes, the light
That creeps from Heaven, just *seems* the stars
  So beautiful and bright."
A moment silent, then I spoke
  Low to the thoughtful child,
"Who told you this, my little maid,
  This story sweet and mild?"

"Why, no one told me," answered she.
  "But how else can it be,
For there's the sky, and there's the stars
  Right up by heaven you see."
All wonderingly, I paused to think,
  But closer to me pressed
The little one, so grave and wise,
  Whose head lay on my breast.

And thought I, "may she not be right,
  More than the learned ones,

Who finds us earthly causes for
    The planets and the suns ? "
And so we sat in silence there,
    The pretty child and I,
And then it seemed all brighter grew
    The stars up in the sky.

And bathed my darling's face in light
    And crowned the golden hair,
What wonder that my thoughts were framed
    That moment in a prayer?

A PERFECT DAY.

[On revisiting the Chapel in which I made my first Communion.]

A BREAST on the surging waters,
    Adrift on the whirlwind, Time,
In the midst of strife and battle
    Echoes a gentle chime ;
A chime, which calls me to dreaming,
    To the shrine where peace gleams fair,
Oh, the music hath brought me reverie,
    And reverie to me, means prayer.

In thought I am back ere Life's storming,
    I am kneeling in incense clouds,
There is never a thought of sorrow,
    There is never a hint of shrouds.

There are white-robed children kneeling,
  White-robed as their soul's array,
And I am one of the favored,
  'Tis my First Communion day.

There's a gleam of white on the altar,
  A miniature Heaven it glows,
And the soul is steeped in rapture,
  For the breath of God o'erflows.
There's a flash of white — the lilies,
  Fragrant, their spotless snow,
And the gold, and waxen tapers
  Are alight, as the blossoms blow.

The music, oh ! how it rises !
  The organ, and voices rare.
And one, that grand contralto
  Bore the soul from the earthland air.
Swayed the censer higher,
  Rose loftier music's tone,
And like a star, the altar
  Out of the incense shone.

But, oh, the boundless rapture
  As my child's soul throbbed with love,
And I seemed in truth, in Heaven
  And I was — for God above
Had come, with His mighty goodness,
  To dwell in my breast that day,
For where God is, there is Heaven,
  As long as He shall stay.

Oh, blest sweet joy and rapture,
  I knew not the clouds above,

With her pretty face all dyed
By the gentle roseate blushes
Which the lilies could not hide —
Idly pulls she there the petals
Of a full-blown crimson rose.

Love's Rose. Page 105.   *Illustration by* J. WILTON CUNNINGHAM.

But God be thanked that I could not,
    And felt but His boundless love.
Oh, God be thanked that I knew not then,
    The gall that my soul must drink,
And God be thanked that He taught me then
    From the Cross I must not shrink.

Oh, happiest day of a life-time
    A day without flaw or cloud,
Nothing can dim its beauty,
    Nothing its joy enshroud.

And brought by that chime I'm kneeling
    Once more, in that Chapel fair.
Once more I a child, am blissful
    In the joy of Communion — prayer.
Around me again the voices,
    Before me the altar there,
And the chime which hath set me dreaming;
    And dreaming like this means prayer.

Abreast on the turbulent ocean,
    Adrift on the winds of time,
I have caught the music which lingers
    And echoes in reverie's chime,
And out of the din and carnage
    And out of the sorrows whirl
The Chapel in sweet St. Vincent's
    Gleams forth like a flawless pearl.

THE SILENT SONG-BIRD.

[In affectionate remembrance of Emma Abbott.]

OH! chill of the Winter, why could you not spare her?
    Why lift the sweet song-bird from out of her nest?
Why freeze with your death-kiss the voice that was sacred?
    Why silence the song, of the heart in her breast?

Oh! chill of the Winter, you surely leave flowers
    Too few in Earth's robe, that you need steal this one;
Too few constellations remain in the heavens;
    Then why dim the Star, which a high place has won?

Oh! chill of the Winter, right royal your sceptre,
    A brave king you came with the crowned New Year.
Then why did you snatch a brave queen from the earthland,
    Whose throne was attained all undaunted by fear?

Oh! chill of the Winter, how could you, how could you,
    Enwrap in your ice arms so awful, so still,
The form of warm genius, the form in whose bosom
    There beat a brave heart ne'er in life knew a chill?

Oh! myriad song-birds, who clustered together,
    And rested within her bright heart to rejoice,
And proud of their home in the full of their gladness,
    Would sing all their gold, through the might of her voice;

Why did ye not, song-birds, when Death came to claim her,
    Sing to the Relentless, your pleading, "Forbear?"
Why did you not woo him to spare her who loved you,
    Nor strike you unvoiceless in very despair?

But even the plea of the song-bird was fruitless ;
　Nor beauty, nor genius may win a reprieve
From that too stern monarch, who turns but an ice-breath,
　And the victim must go, to the arms that receive.

But may we not feel that her sweet voice cleft Heaven,
　And may we not know 'tis not silent—oh, joy !
But has reached a supreme, and an endless forever,
　And won a new honor no death can destroy !

For may we not know that she sings in that Heaven,
　The realm where rise ever loud anthems' grand tone ?
And surely we know that the Star sprang to Angel,
　And God brought His song-bird just nearer His throne.

ADIEU !

[On the departure of His Grace, Archbishop Ryan, for Philadelphia,
and to him affectionately dedicated.]

FROM out our firmament a light is gone,
　That shone in grandeur, for so long a space,
And eastern skies have found another star,
　To deck their midst with its imperial grace.
Our city sighs, as from its mighty arms
　Goes forth, a favored and most noble pride,
When spite of hopes, and prayers to hold him still,
　That gracious boon to her hath been denied.

He rose upon her with his splendid gifts,
　That like a royal sun shot forth a light,
The God-sent gift that in his bosom reigns
　Breathed from his mouth in all its wondrous might.

A king 'mongst orators his words fell clear
    As in the growing night, on flowers drops dew.
Bidding their fragrance lose no purity,
    Lifting the drooping to a life anew.

Anon a fire of diamonds, flashed his tones,
    Their truthful splendor throwing far their light,
Illuming souls with vast magnetic strength,
    And bidding day, spring out from darkened night.
What thousand souls, have felt the mighty fire
    Creep thro' thin space to glow with sacred heat!
What thousand hearts, have felt the soothing balm
    That breathed from words with truth of God replete!

The greatest minds are simple in their strength,
    As children are in innocence' own might;
And, like a child, unconscious of its worth,
    He stands, this soldier of Eternal Right,
God bless him for the truth he taught unto
    Six hundred souls, who died for birthland's good,
Who in the dreary Gratiot prison walls
    Showed Heaven to those who at Death's portals stood.

His dazzling mind is but like light of lamp
    To that supremacy of shining soul,
As meteors that do flash so fitfully,
    Are like the stars that point to God's own goal.

Counselled by one who from the world apart
    Lives sainted life in hidden holiness;
Whose heavenly wisdom taught his soul to spurn
    The glamor of all shallow worldliness—
As Godfrey tossed from off his royal head
    Jerusalem's crown, so Kenrick cast away

All honors save of honoring God alone,
    Which o'er their heads made glory firmer stay.

Oh, happy boon hath been the gift to him
    Who goes from us! To be the trusted friend,
The counselled child who bore that wisdom well,
    And to the world the wondrous shafts did send.
Ah, he must go, despite our tears and pain;
    Go with the blessings crusted and impearled;
Go with the banner of his glowing soul;
    On other hearts its beauties be unfurled.

Go, thousand prayers attend on him, who stood
    By loved ones' bed, to soothe their parting souls,
Whose gentleness, and wisdom lit the way
    Past doubt and agony of Death's dread shoals.
Go, let him flood with liquid tones the souls;
    Flash o'er them truth, in grandeur wide and far;
Let Faith's clear waters shed their crystal streams,
    Impassioned words, each change to heavenly star.

Go. with a mighty chain of hearts entwined,
    Around him linked, by gratitude and love;
And tears shall sacred crystallize to prayers,
    To gem the circlet, sent for him above.
Ah, sad regret that we must lose him now,
    A blessing faded swiftly from our view,
Let others wish him worldly happiness—
    I but commend his soul and life—*Adieu!*

A SORROW'S CROWN.

" This is the truth the poet sings,
   A sorrow's crown of sorrow, is remembering happier things."
                                              —[Tennyson.

I STOOD in the shadows, and watched her to-day
      With her head at rest on her hand so fair,
As she sat in the depths of a window seat
      In the dewy twilight air —
And just like the soft sweet summer rain,
      I saw the tear drops slowly rise
Like a pearly mist, and rest within
      The depths of her soulful eyes.
By the pale sad look on her lovely face
      I knew she was thinking of days a-gone
When she lived in the morning of youth's first dream.
      When her pure young heart was wooed and won,
The old, old story often told
      Yet ever will be again,
For she whom so many had sought to win,
      Had loved — and loved in vain.

He praised her beauty, and called her fair,
      And vowed he'd love her ever and well —
She deemed him all truth, and crowned him king —
      For she lived in the light of a strange sweet spell.
Some trifling act — he called her false —
      They parted ; he went his way.
She seemed so cold, too proud she was
      To turn and bid him stay.
He never dreamed that she loved him thus,
      And, man-like soon forgot

Amid the new faces, and flowers of life —
　　But she — ah, she has not,
And I sighed who knew her story well,
　　As she sat in the depths of the window there —
Thinking unwatched she dreamed alone
　　In the dewy twilight air.

I saw her to-night, but the scene was changed!
　　'Midst music and laughter, and perfumed air
In the ball-room, where gay pleasure ruled,
　　With courtly men, and ladies fair,
She was standing one of the brilliant throng,
　　The gayest of gay admired of all —
Only a word from her beautiful mouth
　　And the proudest man bent at her call —
Clad in a robe of creamy silk,
　　With billowy lace, like the soft sea-foam,
Whilst the gold-brown hair was lightly held
　　In place by a jeweled comb.
Her eyes shone bright, and the carmine glow
　　On her lovely rounded cheek,
Told those, who knew not, a thoughtless belle
　　Who would only pleasure seek.

But I knew that beneath the merry jest,
　　And the laughter gay, and sweet,
Lay heavy and cold her proud young heart,
　　Like the ashes of love at her feet.
Just then from up the crowded stair
　　I saw a handsome man advance —
She saw him, too, with startled look.
　　And cast but one swift glance.
Erect and proud, with a lady bright,
　　Like a frail little snowdrop by his side.

He crossed to where my lady stood,
    And I heard him murmur, "This is my bride."
And she with a glance of calmest friend
    Placed her hand for an instant in his own,
Then turned to his bride and spoke to her
    In a quiet pleasant tone.

She had not thought to see him more —
    She had not heard that he had wed.
Yet, not one word betrayed her pain,
    Or that she scarce knew what she said.
I marveled and thought to myself, "How great
    Are the vasty depths of a woman's heart,
The mysteries and secrets, she holds her own,
    And hides from all with her wonderful art!"
Standing erect 'neath its perfumed weight
    Just by her side stood a slender vase
With splendid poppies, and marguerites fair,
    And lilies tall in their stately grace,
In turning he touched the crystal glass —
    An instant, it lay at my lady's feet,
In quivering fragments, the flowers too,
    Lay dying in fragrance sweet,

A moment before in their living youth
    The bright, sweet flowers of every hue
Stood proud, now broken and crushed they lay.
    Alas, so soon their pride to rue,
With soft regret on his handsome face
    He stooped to pick them from the ground,
When some one called, he turned away ;
    Regret soon passed in the music's sound,
I thought to myself, how strangely like,
    To my lady's life was the vase so pure,

And the flowers too, were the boundless love
    Which only rare women endure.
How her heart, like the vase with the flowers fair,
    Stood fresh and strong in its youthful pride,
One careless touch from his thoughtless hand —
    And the beauty and fragrance died.

I left them there in the brilliant throng —
    The music swelled higher, the laughter rose,
And I turned with a sigh at the outward joy
    And the inward pain that only God knows.

I saw her again when the ball was done
    To-night for a while by the casement stand
In her trailing robe of spotless white
    Like a spirit pale from another land.
But the carmine glow from her cheek had fled,
    And the lustre bright from her soulful eyes.
And I knew she battled with love and life.
    Standing alone, 'neath the starry skies.

I knew she buried the past so fair,
    And crushed the love no longer right;
And I turned and left her standing there
    Alone with her soul, and the deep dark night
Left her there in her peerless beauty,   '
    With her pure young heart in pain and strife
And slowly, I turned to my shadows again,
    For I — I love her better than life.

THE SOUTHLAND POET, ABRAM J. RYAN.

" Merlin said to me,
Some day—some far-off day, when I am dead
You have the simple rhymings of two hearts,
And if you think it best, the world may know
A love-tale crowned by purest sacrifice."
—[Abram J. Ryan.

THE hands that swept the lyre,
  Are strangely quiet now.
The laurel leaves are fadeless
  Above the poet's brow ;
That harp, soft-stringed as twilight,
  Hath fallen at his feet,
Yet echoes all its beauty
  In music sad and sweet.

And ever 'midst our sorrows
  The soothing voice will still,
And ever in our musings
  The gentle words will thrill.

Sweet as though angels breathing
  Through evening silver mist,
Or in their holy missions
  A tired child had kissed,
Fell the sweet poet's solace,
  Framed in each rippling word,
Oftimes as flash of diamond
  The flowing streamlet stirred.

Ah, he who knew poor nature,
  The human good and ill,

Who never touched his lyre
    Save soul-strength to instill;
Who counselled, brave encouraged,
    Lies in the last deep sleep,
Yet, like a corps of angels,
    His songs' sweet vigil keep.

And glorify the silent grave,
    And blazon bright his name,
And love and genius jewel-crown,
    The grand dead poet's fame;
Death drew her solemn curtains round
    The glowing mortal life,
Peace, circled there her legion doves,
    And lo! there ceased all strife.

Oh, glory for the grand, true fame,
    And tears shine for the love,
And as he soothed, so soothe ye all
    In prayers for him above!
Tears, prayers, the rosary of his songs
    Empearl ye, for that name
Which wore the sacred crown of priest
    And won the poet's fame!

Oh, incense, cloud about the grave
    Of hallowed poet-priest,
And breathe a joy that Heaven called
    And mortal woe hath ceased;
Furled is the banner of his life,
    Not conquered,* starred with love,
And gently, holy floats it now
    Triumphant and — above.

---

* "The Conquered Banner" was his best-known poem.

A FRIEND.

GENTLE as silver starlight,
    Fair as a heart-sweet rose,
Bright as the flash of jewel,
    Agleam on sun-kissed snows,
Tender as prayer at even',
    When the Angelus bids us dream,
Like the swift, deep flash of an angel's wing
    As it speeds with golden gleam.

Deep as the rush of the river
    That flows with the year's decree.
Brave as only a woman,
    With a woman's true soul, can be.
Strong, and sweet, and tender,
    Brilliant as flash of sun,
Crowned with rare gifts and graces
    In the gentle soul-world won.

Dear to her friends as a flower,
    Laid in a case of gems
Replete with tender fragrance,
    Yet bright with diadems,
True in her every station,
    Battling to reach her goal.
Flower, in heart and beauty,
    Jewel, in mind and soul.

Sweetest of all this world's gifts,
    A woman, womanly fair,
Seeing the beauties of life-time,
    Scorning its pain, and care,

Loved, and loving, a poem
  In beauty, and pearl-like grace,
Small wonder the sparkling thought-chain
  Has tinted her fair, sweet face.

And left its delicate tracing
  'Neath the wreath of gold-brown hair
Like a song in the bright, fresh morning
  And the echo of some deep prayer.
Thus may the angels find it
  When that other world is won,
As she gives in earth's golden girdle
  That her tireless hands have spun.

A MODERN GALATEA.

SHE swept me by in her silken robes,
  Like a snow queen pure and fair.
One chaliced lily lay amidst
  The sheen of her golden hair,
And on her breast beneath whose snow
  The vestal heart beat high.
In youth and joy, a cluster fair
  In lovely grace did lie,

The favored lilies held their heads,
  All cold, and stately fair,
As though to say " Her virgin heart
  Throbs 'neath us like a prayer,"

And yet with haughty step she swept
  In glistening robes impearled.
One white hand careless toying
  With the fan she oped and furled.

Oh! happy fan, by her caressed,
  Caressing lilies fair,
I envied, till unheeded they
  Fell on the broad, wide stair.
Away she swept, but stooping,
  I raised the buds, and placed
Close hidden o'er my heart for sake
  Of her they late had graced.

The ball is o'er, the music done,
  The hours apace have sped,
I, in my room am musing now
  With lowered eyes and head,
The flaming fire leaps on high
  Until the crimson glow
Warm tints the buds, within my hand
  And dyes their pallid snow.

And I—I clasp them closer still
  And try to pierce the veil,
They hold within their golden hearts,
  And petals chaste and pale.
Sweet lilies, o'er her breast you laid,
  Now whisper, if I dare
But hope, some day my image, too,
  Shall nestle like you there.

For no love thrills this vestal queen,
  She knows not warm desire,

And how may I dare hope to light
    The high and holy fire.
But yet, you tell me, once when I
    Bowed o'er her hand, you felt
Her heart throb higher. Blessed thought,
    Some day the snow may melt!

And see the night give place to dawn,
    Whose dimpled smile, and pink,
May bear me on Hope's swift-winged barque
    To Love's deep rapturous brink.

So glides, my lady in her pearls,
    Before my mind to-night,
And I in reverie's happy sway
    Warm kiss the lilies white.
Great heavens! Like their petals, I
    Grow pale, as now they are,
For I forgot when dreaming thus
    To banish my cigar.

How rude — I doff apology's
    Plumed cap, queen, as you sweep
In proud unconsciousness my mind,—
    And now I'm off to sleep.

AN ANSWER.

WHAT shall I write to you, dear ;
    Since you have asked for a word ?
Speech is not easy to come
    When hearts are like mine deeply stirred.
Dear, but your message to-day
    Flew like a dove on the wing,
Fell like a dew drop of light   .
    On a too early rose of the Spring.

Oh, but the scroll of my past
    Lies in my mind all unrolled.
Oh, but my thought artist's brush,
    Paints now her picture of gold.
I remember how brightly the time
    Sped with us, once, in its flight.
How we saw only royal day's sun,
    And the silver of stars in the night.

How our laughter ran, blithe as a deer
    At play, near a bright crystal spring.
How we cared not to plot, or to plan,
    Sufficient each day that took wing.
Dear, how we drifted apart
    Drifted in sorrow and tears,
Trusting our sweet ship of hope
    Would bring back our treasure in years.

And then how new aims filled our lives,
    And memory grew dimmer each day,
We were but human you know,
    And that the world's usual way.

Tears are falling moist and gentle
From the great heart of the sky.
* * * * * *

Nature, like a woman sobbing,
Weeps out all her care and pain.

A Rainy Day. Page 197.   *Illustration by* PAUL CORNOYER.

And scarce ere we knew it our love
    Changed to a dream that lay dead,
Friendship sprang up from the grave
    New blossoms to deck her fair head.

And now, dear, how vain are the words
    You have asked me to write you to-day,
When one heart, but echoes a heart,
    Ah, then there is nothing to say.
You are content, so you write
    Dear, I am glad that 'tis so,
There is no need to affect
    The feeling we had long ago.

We are so changed, you and I,
    'Tis better, resigned that we be,
To the fate that once seemed so stern,
    The breakers that buried love's sea,
You are content, ah, dear friend,
    Yours is the happier part,
And I — well — if tears aught reveal,
    Still I have left me a heart.

Not for the love which is dead,
    Changed to a fairer cold clay,
No, I have banished all that,
    And live in the world's garish day,
You are content now at last,
    I, battling for that which I crave,
Well, in the end which is best?
    We'll know it, dear, after the grave.

AD MAJOREM DEI GLORIAM.

[Suggested by a religious procession passing through the streets.]

SLOWLY the chain of life passed by,
    Swelled the music in proud proclaim,
Flashed the gleaming banners aloft,
    Raised to the honor of One Great Name.
A splendid thread of human hearts,
    A smile of glory, a gleaming thought,
A panorama of glowing souls,
    A massive picture of beauty wrought.

" All for the greater glory of God,"
    Nations commingling passed my sight;
Strife and discord lulled to rest
    Under the banner of yellow and white.
Rank and station were counted not,
    Nothing but souls in the mighty train;
Marching in ardor and zeal they gleamed
    In this beautiful era of progress' reign.

Chargers pranced to the music's strains,
    Glittered gay colors beneath the sun;
A rainbow of beauty, a curve of grace,
    A living prayer to the Glorious One.
Robed in their purple the bishops passed,
    · Simply they sat in majestic grace;
The minds of grandeur, and souls sublime,
    Throwing their lights over each grand face.

" All for the greater glory of God,"
    Slowly the stream of souls flash on;

Thus may they pass into Heaven some day,
    Greeting the King whose armor they don.
Race and color, station and rank,
    Forgot in the honor of soul's delight;
Nations commingling hand in hand,
    Under the banner of yellow and white.

A CHORD IN THE MUSIC.

GLOW of poppies, and diamonds' gleam,
    Glimmer of eyes, and hair,
A mist of lace and a paradise
    In the alcove under the stair.
Rustle of silk, and sway of fan,
    Ripple of laughter gay,
Words as warm as the poppies hear
    When the sun-god speeds his way.

Soft breathed vows and transports light,
    Joy shrugs her shoulder at sorrow,
To-night, in our kingdom under the stair;
    Where shall we be on the morrow?
Smiles on her lips for another one.
    Women grow weary, you know, they say,
If the faces change not, on which they smile
    When the night melts into the day.

And women are not alone, I vow,
    What men crave most is change.
We have no time in this life of whirl
    To think some things are strange.

Let us alone, two play at the game,
   We must bask in the candle's light,
And what care we for to-morrow's pain,
   In the bliss of the gay to-night?

"Come, ma reine, ere the music's o'er,
   This pulsing waltz I'll claim.
What! Is our heaven already done?
   Your card has another name!
I'm promised too, by my knightly word,
   This dance I had nigh forgot
In the smiles of your beautiful presence here,
   And the spell of this lonely spot."

"Let me keep this bud, when you take your fan
   For that other one to sway.
Ah, you smile, fair cynic, and ask me where
   The flower will fade away.
"On my word,"—but she's gone, and the flower's tossed,
   Good heavens, where did it fall!
It caught on her train, as she threw it down,
   And she's swept it out of the hall.

I'd like to have kept it one night at least,
   With her breath, on its petals still,
But the waltz beats high, and I must not think
   Or the music will wear a chill.
Glow of poppies, and diamonds' gleam,
   Pleasure speed on thy way,
But oh! what the angels in heaven record
   For the slaves of a fashion's day.

LOVE'S DREAM

SONG.

I WILL not blame you, but adieu;
  From you fore'er I go.
For I have built my throne of Love,
  Within a heart of snow.
Alas! how brilliant my love dream,
  As golden-bright as brief
To me it was a scroll of life
  To you a careless leaf.

REFRAIN.

  To me it was a scroll of life.
  To you a careless leaf.
  To you a careless leaf.

But oh! those glowing kisses then,
  That made a heaven for me
Now burn with all the restless heat
  Of fierce Love's memory.
Adieu! adieu! my dream has fled,
  Life's trees are bleak and bare
I go, but oh, the pain to know,
  No soft regret you share.

REFRAIN.

  I go, but oh, the pain to know
  No soft regret you share.
  No soft regret you share.

CROWNED.

TO MRS. G. H. L.

STATELY, and calm, and gracious,
With lights in the deep, dark eyes,
Like stars, that have fallen to earthland,
Adown from the cloudless skies.
With tender lights in the shadows,
With liquid love in their gleams;
Where the soul of a lofty purpose
Has fallen asleep in dreams.

Where the soul of a noble woman
Shines forth, in resolve's grand truth;
Where the reign of a gentle spirit
Wins the fadeless charm of youth;
Where the wise, and the good, and gentle
Are shrined in the love-filled space;
Ah! those eyes are the eyes, whose lustre
Glows in the fair, sweet face.

With her mind a sparkling jewel,
She hath lighted the way by truth;
And the stars of a perfect splendor
Shall shine in an always youth.
And the beads of life, she telleth,
'Neath the hope of religion's sway,
And the rainbow that spans in promise
Is lighting in grace her way.

As a "valiant woman" she standeth,
And blessed may she ever be,
Wherever her spirit dwelleth,
On earth or eternity!

THE DRUID'S BANNER.*

QUEEN SCOTIA stands amidst her dazzling train,
    Her regal arm upholds her banner high,
The brazen serpent gleaming in its coils
    Floats proudly out, beneath Hispania's sky.
'Tis the same serpent, which long years ago
    Nial of Scythia in the desert sought
With sick Gadelius, who, embraced its form,
    And rose full healed, by the great good it wrought.
Then quoth Prince Nial, "In gratitude, my tribe
    To the great serpent, whom my son did save,
Beneath its form our battles shall be won,
    On our blest banner shall it henceforth wave."

Thus was that banner, consecrated there,
    The sacred emblem of the Celtic train,
The favored symbol of the Druid's faith.
    That shone ne'er brighter, than in Scotia's reign.
So as she stands, high on the vine-wreathed hills,
    Her dusky hair encircled by the crown
Of the proud Celts, she issues a command,
    Sprung from her wisdom, which has won renown ;
One Druid bard stands pliant at her will,
    With harp which skillful hands now lightly string,
And with sweet voice proclaims unto the tribe
    The queen s command. These words the Druids sing:

QUEEN SCOTIA'S SONG.

" Fair is Hispania's sunny land, my tribe,
    But prophet's tell of fairer hill and vale ;

---

* Upon the introduction of Christianity into Ireland — A. D. 433.

The land of destiny lies westward still—
　　On, Celts, to find the promised Innisfail !

"There grasses gleam, like jewels in my crown.
　　There cool streams flow, as clear as our own glass ; *
There flowers peep forth, each like a fairy face,
　　And fairy harps play in the winds that pass.

"The azure skies are flecked with rose and gold,
　　The Sun-god throws o'er all a dazzling veil,
The air is scented by a perfumed breath
　　That seeks for kisses from our Innisfail.

"There shall our Druids find their sacred trees,
　　There shall our bards feel sweet, delicious song,
There shall my halls of marble, white arise,
　　There shall my people triumph over wrong.

"The land of destiny lies westward yet.
　　Farewell, Hispania, ere three moons grow pale
Our sacred banner shall float proudly out,
　　Beneath the skies of promised Innisfail ! "

Ah ! Innisfail, 'tis found ! The Celtic eye
　　Hath drank its beauty, with enraptured gaze ;
And Scotia's arm unfolds her banner high,
　　And, Celtic bards break forth in songs of praise.
Ah, verdant land, 'tis fairer than a dream.
　　An emerald gem, it rises from the sea,
And Scotia cries, "Our destiny is found ! "
　　No fairer Innisfail, than this, could be,

---

* The Phœnicians were the discoverers of glass-making.

High in the breeze, the Celtic banner floats.
    'Neath giant oaks the Druids' rites begin,
Thus under Scotia, and her sacred flag
    The Celts' possession of fair Erin win.

*   *   *   *   *   *   *

Swift Time hath woven many changing strands,
    And Scotia sought her native dust again ;
Yet proud as when her queenly arm unfurled,
    The sacred banner, floats o'er Laighaire's reign ;
Still in the elements the Druids seek
    For the great Being, whom they yearn to know.
Still priest and priestess, in their sacred groves,
    Invoke vague worship, as in long ago,
Unconscious that more near, each passing day
    Time's waves are swiftly bearing Faith's bright light,
Which shall like fire consume the dark belief,
    And Druidism darken into night.

'Tis Easter eve, tho' Druids know it not,
    But honor as a feast, the natal day
Of kingly Laighaire,* who in old Tara's halls
    Hath round the throne, his court in proud array.
The dark-robed Druids, solemn grouped about ;
    The prophets placed in honor, near the king ;
The warriors gleaming in their armor bright,
    And bards with lyres, that echo while they sing.
Near the great monarch in his purple, rests
    His blue-eyed queen in 'broidered robes of gold,
Her graceful head, above the fair hair's sheen,
    A crown of diamonds, doth like stars uphold.

---

* Pronounced Lear.

Outspoke the grand Arch-Druid to his king:
    "O Laighaire, all fires are quenched thro' Celtic land,
And all is dark as night, that is unstarred,
    Till for a signal thou shalt raise thy hand,
Then shall be waved the flame, whose sacred power
    Shall at the once restore all fires to light,
For no great feast save of our monarch's birth
    Should Celtic eye behold the wondrous sight!"
True speaks the Druid, for the gloaming rests,
    Deepened and dark, with not one gilded ray.
For swiftest death is his who dares to burn
    His fire on this, the noble monarch's day.

But lo! what's that, that flashes through the air,
    What brilliant glare like light of noon-tide sun?
What gleams cleave thro' the mist of Tara's halls,
    Until the kingly throne of Laighaire is won?
Up springs the monarch, mighty in his wrath.
    "Who dares the gods! what traitor have we here?
The vile blasphemer ere an hour shall die!
    Guards seize the man who thus defies King Laighaire!"
"O monarch! ruler of the Celtic land,"
    So spake a Druid prophet, loud and clear,
"On yonder hill, there burns a fire this eve,
    If not now quenched, shall burn forever here!"

"Ha! say'st thou thus! Then by the winds, and sun
    Yon blasphemer, shall know what king doth reign!
On, till we quench at once his fire and life!
    On, to the desecrated hill of Slane!"
As fast as lightning cleaves the stormy sky,
    The chariots dash across the Celtic plain,
The Druid warriors led by king and queen,
    A flash of fire, a dazzling, splendid chain.

Unmindful of the coming storm, the fire
    Flashes and glows, defining in its rays
A silent group, whilst one tall regal form
    Stands fearless forth, in waiting as he prays.

'Tis he! The traitor whom the monarch seeks!
    Ah! can a traitor stand so proudly there?
Ah! can a traitor wear so grand a face,
    Sublime with faith and christian-courage rare?
'Tis the great Gaul, now Ireland's patron saint,
    Who fearless burns his Paschal fire, this eve,
Filling the destiny, that thro' his voice
    The Celtic souls shall the true faith receive.
Before the waiting saint, Laighaire's chariot stops,
    "Speak, traitor! Why this blasphemy is done.
For thou shalt pay this daring deed with death
    Before to-morrow shines our worshipped sun!"

In bishop's robes, and crozier of his rank,
    Stands Patrick there, and raising high his hand
Cries, "I will speak, and tell the only truth,
    Not at thine, Laighaire's, but at my God's command,
The words of truth flow forth, like liquid gold,
    And glow like fire upon each listener's ear.
Faith throws its shadows, softly o'er their souls,
    The God they sought, 'tis he of whom they hear."
Truth slowly dawns to all, save to King Laighaire,
    He bids his priests defy the traitor Gaul.
His will is theirs. On sky, and sun, and winds,
    And worshipped things for aid they vainly call.

Loud prays the saint, unto the only God,
    Bright, brighter flashes to the evening skies
The Paschal fire, emitting gleams of truth
    That in each heart to christian fires arise.

By wondrous works the only faith is proved
    To Druids, prophets, and the bards, most clear,
And in their train the Celts and warriors kneel
    Save but a group, that clusters nearer Laighaire.
From the king's side speeds forth the Celtic queen,
    Her haughty face, now soft with faith so rare,
With golden tresses streaming in the winds,
    At Patrick's feet, she throws herself in prayer.

Pale, startled, sobbing like a timid maid, .
    She prays the saint to bless her kneeling there.
With words he soothes her as he would a child,
    And rests one hand upon the soft gold hair.
Like lion raging, stands King Laighaire at bay,
    And high aloft the serpent emblem waves:
"My tribe, behold the banner of our faith.
    This sacred flag great Druidism saves,
Our fathers fought beneath its mighty folds,
    Our people prospered well until this day.
Oh! Druids, warriors, will ye basely now
    Your king and sacred banner thus betray?"

Peace! — Slow the saint doth raise his holy staff,
    Pointing to where the brazen emblems glow;
Behold! The banner springs from Laighaire's grasp,
    And lies half buried in the earth below.
And lo! that moment every serpent there
    With venom deadened plunged into the sea.
And from that eve, all Celtic soil hath been
    From reptiles, and from Druidism free.
Low lies the banner of the Druids' faith,
    Hid in the deep, and starless dark of night,
Yet flashes with its waves of green and gold
    The Christian banner of eternal right.

AN EASTER SONG.

THE sun has opened its casket,
    And broadcast flung each gem,
To dazzle with light, and glory bright,
    And shower his rays with them.
The flowers' sweet tender faces
    Have caught the golden dye,
And the filmy mist of the clouds sun-kissed
    Drape soft the sapphire sky.

The bells of the Christian earthland
    Are raised in a proud proclaim,
And each silver voice in her favored choice,
    Calls aloud the Holy Name.
The world her form upraising
    From the penance posture low,
Her voice is flinging, her words are ringing
    That dear God loves us so

Oh, Christ hath risen, hath risen,
    All christian souls upraise,
For the dazzling ray of the grand sweet day,
    Your souls in a deep-felt praise,
In praise of the great Creator :
    In praise for His love so rare,
And echo the peal, and gently kneel,
    For His tender love and care.

Blow Easter lilies in beauty !
    In fragrant silence sway,
And in love intense, waft your incense
    On this glorious Easter day !

Oh Christ hath risen, hath risen,
  Oh, joy, oh, Heavenly light,
Peal silver bell, with each note tell
  That the day crowns always night.

PHILOSOPHY.

RARE roses bright, in joy's delight,
  Bloom oft in loneliest places,
And shoals unseen, with dreary mien
  Uprise, in sun-lit spaces.

Oft storms sweep o'er, the flowered floor
  Of stately, gracious castle,
And stray sun-beams, dance with gay gleams
  O'er some imprisoned vassal.

Oft rainbow spans a lonely sky,
  Where eye dwells never on it,
And some sweet dove, or bird of love,
  Breathes, where none hears the sonnet.

Thus grief, and joy, and grace alloy,
  Are found where least expected,
And next in grace, to cottage space,
  ' A palace is erected.

We never know, what winds may blow,
  Or what to-morrow's weather,
So, drink them all, the wine and gall,
  Wear rose and thorn together.

A MON BIEN-AIMÉ.

I BREATHED a kiss on the winds, to-day,
  And begged them soft to blow thy way,
And take the kiss that I blew on them,
A kiss that was rarer than any gem —
To my lover, the one that I hold so dear,
To thee, my love, for thou wert not near.

I breathed a sigh on a flower bright,
A purple pansy, bathed in sunlight,
I plucked the flower, and threw it high,
And prayed it fall with my gentle sigh
Across the path, where thy feet would tread ;
For they'd feel thee near did they both lie dead.

I sent a wish by a star, to-night,
A star, that shone with a wondrous light,
And I cried, "Oh, star, with your tranquil rays,
Light my lover's path with your golden haze ;
Shine on him, e'en tho' he should not know,
That you fill his path, with a radiant glow ! "

I knelt in pleading prayer, to-night,
Before God, whose holy will is might,
And I prayed from the depths of my loving heart
That He would allot thee a noble part,
That His tender hand, from the throne above,
Would guide the path of my own dear love.

BRIDAL CHIMES.*

OH! the stars on the banner are gleaming,
    In glory a thousand times bright,
For the flag of our country is waving
    O'er the President's bridal to-night.
Sweet Liberty's goddess is smiling
    Aloft from her pedestal fair,
And her smiles form a halo of blossoms
    To crown the girl-bride's silken hair.

Oh! the eagle is spreading in glory
    His wings o'er these nuptials of love;
Oh, Democracy's arch is brave spanning
    As she guards him in triumph above;
And the stars of the heavens are gemming
    The sky with a radiance bright,
And they whisper to each silver sister,
    "'Tis the President's bridal to-night!"
And the moon sweeps her vestures all queenly,
    Creeping slow o'er America's skies,
For she lingers above those two plighting
    Their troth, while she steals in their eyes.

Oh, a nation is earnest deep praying
    For the one they trust, honor and love,
And a million heart-throbs are ascending
    For our Cleveland to God high above.
Oh, the orange buds sway in their sweetness,
    And say, "we are honored in might;
Our kingdom is climaxed in glory
    For we're ruling a ruler to-night."

---

* Upon the wedding day of Grover Cleveland, President
of the United States, and Miss Frances Folsom.

With golden tresses streaming in the winds,
    At Patrick's feet, she throws herself in prayer.
Pale, startled, sobbing like a timid maid,
    She prays the saint to bless her kneeling there.

The Druid's Banner. Page 140.   *Illustration by* ANDRE BOWLES.

Flash the flag of our country in splendor
 O'er the one who upholds it in right!
Whose hands grasp the colors like iron,
 Whose rule is as true as 'tis bright.
Gleam, oh stars, in your sky's azure banner
 Throw soft o'er two hearts' holy glow,
Still twine with a vague chain of silver
 When to-night shall be classed "long ago."

But oh, angels, I pray, kneel, dear angels,
 In pleading to that king above,
That He will bless ever and smile on
 Our President's nuptials and love.
Democracy stand all in armor
 For God has willed all of your might,
And waft high an anthem of grandeur
 O'er our President's bridal to-night.

A TRIBUTE.

TO THE MEMORY OF THE LATE HON. SAMUEL T. GLOVER.

O SNOWS of winter, I do pray ye fall
 Gently, to cover on this earth below
His new-made grave, until the flowers come
 To take your place, and breathe their softened woe.
O bitter winds, I bid ye cease your strife,
 Blow softly as ye whirl about that place;
Moan if ye will, but tearful, prayerful moans,
 Until spring breezes sob their tender grace.

O gentle moon, throw from your silvery throne
 A chastened glow, to light the quiet spot;

Oh sun, shed not too warm nor faint your rays,
    And tender stars, ye will forget him not.
O rains, if ye must come, fall soft and slow,
    Let your moist tears keep fresh and sweet the grass;
O noiseless dew, gem with your twice day pearls,
    And birds, rest here to sing before ye pass.

O trees, I do entreat that ye will fling
    Your shadows softly, where he lies at rest;
For know ye all, here lies a nature's king,
    One who did wield life's sceptre for the best,
And marble, when ye gleam above his head,
    Press lightly in your strength upon the sod;
Stand like a sentinel to tell the years
    Here lieth one who lived and died in God.

Ah, woe, for he is dead, if death means that
    He is forever lost to earth and love;
Dead, if it means the grand and noble heart
    Hath ceased to throb, commanded from above.
Dead, if it means the high and gifted mind
    No more shall marvel on the theme of life;
Dead, if it be the brave, and generous soul
    Shall bend no more in pain or earthly strife.

Dead, if the kindly, and the tireless hands
    Are folded, now, above the pulseless heart,
That beat so nobly in its every throb —
    That bowed to God, and won eternal rest;
Dead, if these things be death, but ah, he lives,
    Where earth-life ends, and glory is beyond,
Unending day, a vast eternal song —
    A crown of Heaven, the blameless life hath won.

MOONLIGHT.

A SONG.

SOFT moonlight, is flooding the earthland, to-night,
    With silvery wonder, and glorious gleams.
And it casts o'er me mem'ries, that still and subdue me,
    Bathing my soul in the tenderest dreams.
Dreams of the night, when was whispered thy love,
    Soft in the moonlight, my darling to me,
When I lived 'neath the ardor of passionate words,
    And felt that the world held no other, than thee.

But the beautiful night, and the passionate words,
    Are gone like some glories, that shone but a while:
Still the moonlight, caresses and kisses the earth,
    But to me only mem'ry is left of love's smile.
My darling, my darling, ah can'st though forget
    The night in the moonlight, thou wander'dst with me!
Tho' our paths lie apart now, and must be forever,
    I live but, my darling, in dreaming of thee!

Oh, moonlight caress me, and throw round thy veil
    Of silverlike glory, I revel in thee;
For I know he is thinking, when watching thy beauty,
    Of her who will ever his faithful love be.
What care I for fate, or for long separation
    E'en tho' he think himself false unto me,
For our hearts are enwoven with chains, firm yet tender,
    Some day in some life, he will come back to me.

WHO MAY KNOW.

SHE stood upon a lonely stretch of sand;
 Before her rolled the sullen angry sea,
A shadow, of a cross, shot 'thwart the sky,
 A shadow, in her eyes, gloomed hopelessly.

Lo, in the distance clear, a white speck rose,
 A coming ship; her dark eyes flashed with light,
Hope's messenger. "'Tis come," she cried,
 "To tell that day has triumphed over night."

Thundered the billows, yet she strained her eyes.
 Nearer it came, the white-winged ship to her;
Down on her knees she fell in ecstacy,
 And bowed her head, too thrilled with joy to stir.

"'Tis come, 'tis come at last, oh light-house kind,
 To guide my ship past rocks, so pale and wan!"
Proudly she raised her head, and swept her gaze,
 Out towards the coming ship,—just God! 'twas gone.

Thundered the billows. Dark the sullen sky.
 The shadow of the cross grew deeper still;
It fell upon a woman lying there,
 Upon a sweet face, strangely pale and chill.

Thundered the billows. Lo, a white star gleamed
 Where rose the ship, that seemed a mirage light.
That seemed, I say, for who dare say that Death
 Is not the day, that triumphs over night.

A GOLDEN SPRAY.*

FIFTY years ago, the sunlight
    Gleamed all golden in its flow,
Rare illuming youth's sweet pathway
    With its mighty radiant glow.
'Neath the golden lights, sweet flowers,
    Sprang all magic in their dew,
Spangling with their dreamy fragrance,
    Perfuming two hearts so true.

Golden weather! golden sunlight!
    Golden harps, sweet stringed with love!
Not one cloud to mar the sapphire
    Of the spotless sky above.
But as years crept by, the starlight
    Swept away its radiant glow;
Only stars of misty silver,
    O'er the two heart-worlds did glow.

Then the starlight lost its silver;
    One sweet world, felt Death's dark cloud;
One brave heart, grew hushed and silent
    'Neath the dreary awful shroud,
And that other wept in darkness,—
    Weeping for life's happy gold,
Weeping that the other heart-life
    Lay too silent, hushed, and cold.

'Neath the marble cross, cold—gleaming,
    In his southern grave he lies,

---

* Written for a friend, on the fiftieth anniversary of
her wedding day.

Yet his loved one's prayers will pass. it,
    And cleave far above the skies—
Cleave, and crystallize in Heaven.
    God is ever tender—kind;
Every pleading prayerful heart throb
    Heard, and answered she will find.

When her chastened spirit, gladly
    Kneels in happiness supreme;
Then she'll know that each dark earth cloud
    Held within a golden gleam.
Ah! brave bear—life's but a feather,
    Blowing light, and swift away.
We're but born, to know the twilight,
    Night comes always after day.

Ah, but bear, true life's to come yet,
    In that Heaven again, those two
All the golden of their youth's love;
    Thrice the golden, will renew;
Then rare flowers will deck them sweetly,
    Crystals fresh, prayer's holy dew,
And God's grand love will perfume
    Hearts His love so deeply knew—

God but chastens those He loves well,
    And who bears each earthly loss
Bravely will he be rewarded—
    Gem for tear, and crown for cross.
Tears are love, and love is holy;
    Stars in resignation's sky,
Form a halo of grand glory,
    Greets the sorrowful on high.

A CROWN.

[On the birthday of my mother.]

THY birthday, oh, thy birthday!
　　One more to mark the years,
That glinted thy soft rippling hair,
　　As though with silvered tears.
That placed upon its beauty
　　Those moonbeams, there to gleam
In all their gentle splendor,
　　Like sad, and softened dream.

When joy did smile upon thee,
　　Thy locks were raven hue,
They matched thy brown eyes beauty,
　　Loved eyes so sweet and true.
The raven hue hath vanished,
　　Left with thy joy, and youth,
Yet dear, we hold thy silver
　　The fairest hair, in truth.

It tells of sorrows borne,
　　It breathes of anguished days,
When death thy heart had blighted,
　　And tangles wrapped thy ways.
It tells of duties bravely done,
　　Of more than mother's love;
A crown of silver, thine on earth,
　　A crown of gold above.

DULCIE.

WHAT a dainty little lady,
  What a faultless *riante* face,
What deep eyes, of wine-brown splendor,
  In their chaliced beauty's space ;
What a trim, and perfect figure,
  What a calm, and high-bred air,
What a brow, like alabaster,   .
  Just as white, and free from care.

What fair skin, the tint of sea-shell,
  What bright hair, the throne of gold,
And what moulded little snowflakes,
  Do the pretty slippers hold.
What a smile, serene and gracious,
  What a manner of repose,
What a mouth, just formed for kisses,
  And oh, what a charming nose.

Toute ensemble, she is a fairy,
  Winsome with a sweet delight,
She was born to be a blessing,
  In that tranquil beauty bright,
Born for sunshine, and for smiling,
  To chase every tear away,
Even her birthday was the sweetest
  Òne on earth. 'Twas Christmas Day.

Better still, no word unkindly
  Barbed will ever pass her lips.
Never until day is over,
  Will her sunshine know eclipse.

What though no career's before her,
 Fame in poesy, or art,
What though no dramatic brilliance;
 For a social star's her part.

Still reclined in willow carriage,
 Silken robed in pink, and lace,
Shall admiring throngs surround her.
 Praising loud her peerless grace.
Even now there stands a lover,
 All devotion in blue eyes.
Bends above to sue her favor,
 Like a star-gleam from the skies.

Such absorbing love, and homage
 Never queen has won before,
Bending o'er the dreamy beauty
 Love unclasps his magic door.
Oh, this lover knows that never
 Glance unkind, will cloud her face,
Never change of fickle passion.
 In this faithful love find place.

Who, you ask, are maid and lover?
 What perfections thus enthrall?
Little Constance is the lover,
 Dulcie is—her cherished doll.

THY FIRST COMMUNION DAY.

IN clouds of tulle about thy form,
        And spotless veil of grace,
With crown of lilies o'er thy brow,
        And peace lights on thy face,
Great roses filling little hands,
        That clasp them soft in prayer,
The outward symbols of true joy,
        Like incense in the air.

Sweet child, behold the Altar's gleam,
        And candles' waxen glow,
With just beyond wide banks of fern,
        Upholding buds like snow.
All fair and gold, the chapel's space,
        The censer sways aloft.
And with the fragrant mist there comes,
        A Benediction soft.

But e'en these attributes of grace,
        Show ill the joys that shine,
And flood thy childish soul, until
        The human grows divine;
For in thy breast, this sacred day,
        The King of Kings hath deigned,
To visit, first thy chastened soul,
    `   And in its midst hath reigned.

So when He entered in that spot,
        That soul all freed from sin,
A thousand angels to adore,
        In rapture crowded in,

And Heaven above took up the song
    And said "This child is blessed,
For God hath given His grandest gift—
    Himself, within her breast!"

Oh, grandeur great, oh, joy sublime,
    Louise, hath come to thee,
Oh, let the blessing never cease
    But bring Eternity.
No wealth the world could ever send,
    No fame, or throne, or joy,
But brings a shadow in its train ;
    E'en sun-beams, clouds destroy.

For these are human, but, my child
    The gift that is Divine,
Is fadeless in ecstatic bliss,
    And this to-day is thine.
And when temptations cross thy way
    With brilliant lurid gleam,
Oh, turn from them to this rare time,
    When earth was Heaven's dream.

And this my prayer: no worldly joys
    I crave for thee, but, oh,
May thou appear in Heaven as now,
    In spotless robes of snow!

HER SECRET.

I LISTENED to them prattling,
    The pretty maidens there,
Praising his perfect beauty,
    Of eyes, and sunlit hair.
And each one marked the power,
    His voice could soft beguile.
But only one, said nothing   ˙
    Yet listened with a smile.

I heard them marvel earnestly
    If ever he did love,
Or if it hovered o'er him now
    A rose-tint from above.
Then each grew pensive,
    And thoughful for the while,
But one sat strangely silent
    Yet dreaming with a smile.

I knew she heard the voices,
    Like zephyrs far away,
Or silver-sparkling fountains
    That plash in gentle May.
Or some sweet music breathing,
    Of love naught can defile,
Low drooped her eyes of topaz,
    Bright tinted with a smile.

I knew her heart was whispering,
    Back to her gentle soul,
How out beneath the starlight,
    That heart had reached its goal.

How with his rapturous kisses,
    Of whom they spoke the while,
She learned life's sweetest lesson,
    And listened with a smile.

A TRIBUTE TO COLONEL P. S. GILMORE.

ORPHEUS lulled by his wondrous harp
    And charmed by his soothing lyre.
But Gilmore rouses each throbbing heart,
    And fills our souls with fire,
With every tone of pulsing strains
    Wakes echoes strong and clear,
And the master's hand moves ever on
    To joy and hopeful cheer.

In all the countless human hearts,
    Vast waves of human lives
He cleaves the sea to grasp the pearls
    And safe with them arrives.
A grand interpreter of Souls,
    A mystic Bard of sound,
He climbed the people's hearts and stood
    A victor on his ground.

He throws with lavish hand amongst
    All wounded hearts brave cheer,
And in the magic of his notes
    Each heart forgets its tear.

He feels the value of a smile,
    The might of joy, and strength,
He gauges people's craved-for wants
    And spans all true their length.

Like gentle balm to weary breasts,
    He sends his grand sweet strains,
And joy, and grief, and youth and age
    Each finds his golden gains.
God's love he teaches, joy and faith
    He shows his grandest gifts,
And like a prophet sent, he stands,
    And Sorrow's curtain lifts.

He teaches joy, and life and day,
    Bright glory, hope and fame,
A brilliant meteor dawned on earth,
    When Gilmore to her came.
May blessings cluster 'round his life
    For all the good he wrought,
And win him Heaven's laurels, for
    The grand and true he taught.

Fame lights her tapers o'er his name,
    But Love cleaves deeper still,
And every heart and every breast,
    A space for him shall fill.

                        —October, 1890.

MISSOURI.*

PROUDLY she stands, the brave young Queen of West
    And points aloft her grand on urging hand,
Beckoning the world to send her armies on,
    Led by young Progress to the lofty stand.
In liquid might her mantle flows about
    Her shoulders, and the giant stream that runs,
Sweeps her fair beauty in its mighty rush,
    And throws aloft the glitter of her suns.
Oh, mantle Mississippi, great in strength,
    Wondrous in might, oh, vast and peerless river,
Right well you deck the massive picture world,
    Oh, mighty gift from the Almighty Giver!
The world fit wedded to grim staunch old Time,
    Caresses ever this their child of age
And Fame opes wide her book and glowing writes,
    MISSOURI, golden on its proudest page.

Around her grouped her courtiers, forests green,
    And smiling cavaliers, the sweeping plains,
Cascades coquetting with the changing skies,
    And misty bluffs, like warders shield her gains.
The Iron King has sought the glowing Queen,
    And laid his tributes at her proud young feet,
Lead's kingdom here took up his lordly rule,
    And generous nature made her gift complete.
Like some dark prince uprises Pilot Knob,
    Eager to make his devoirs, and to guard
His sovereign liege, and lady. Sentinel
    He stands majestic and unyielding in regard.

---

* In the Missouri Historical Society's album, St. Louis, 1886.

Arcadia, brightest princess, with her train
    Of laughing sprites pay homage fair and gay;
Barbaric relics valued from their age,
    Mark savage overthrow, and Christian sway.

And deeper, lonelier in their grand true strength,
    The crosses rise at intervals in state,
Marking the footsteps of Religion's tread,
    The silent symbols God's love did create.
Like gems that sparkle on her pulsing breast,
    Gleam flashing diadems of buildings rare,
And towers float their brilliance to the sky,
    Renown proclaims them great beyond compare.
But stars within this star world gently shine
    To deck the brave queen's God-directed space,
And from her heart there gleams and sparkles bright,
    A myriad gem, thrice-honored Genius' face.

Behold the Artist WIMAR, greatest soul,
    And gifted far beyond each gifted son.
Cloud-dark his life, true life sprang out of death,
    And deathless fame Missouri's genius won.
Behold our EADS, whose giant brain sent forth
    The wonders of the jetties, and the bridge,
Whose worthy name shines luminous afar,
    And spanned high-reaching Fame's stupendous ridge.
And that philanthropist, who modest tried
    To hide his deeds, yet sent they forth their glow,
And though against his will, posterity
    Shall honor, bless the name of WAYMAN CROW.

A thousand faces, literature and art,
    The martyr-missionary, best of all,

Gleam, glow, and sparkle with their wondrous light,
    Springing in answer to their summoned call,
    *   *   *   *   *   *   *   *
Names, fames, and souls in swift succession speed,
    To form the gems brave, flashing round her mien,
And in America's vast monarchy:
    MISSOURI, reigns a God-blessed crowned Queen.

"PER ASPERA AD ASTRA."

A H! why did'st wake me? For I was in truth,
    Lost in a sweet, and strange absorbing dream.
A fantasy so wondrous, that it leaves
    Me dazed, bewildered, by its lifelike gleam.
I thought I stood within a vast expanse,
    Above there shone a cloudless sky of blue;
The ground a velvet mantle wore of moss,
    'Broidered with flowers, that on its bosom grew.

'Mid rainbow tints, each held a golden eye,
    Enframed in petals of bright varied hue,
Wafting such fragrance with their gentle breaths,
    That fairy tears alone, could be the dew
That fell on them, in crystals morn and eve,
    To keep them ever moist, and pure, and fair.
The hidden power so great, it thrilled my mind,
    As clouds of incense mingle with our prayer.

I threw myself reclining on the moss;
    Within the flowers' hearts I hid my face,
'Till sweetest transports swept across my soul.
    Forgetting all lost in their depths of grace,

In the soft pleasure of my tender rest.
    A languor crept like that of gentle love,
'Till all was called to throbbing flushing life,
    By a sweet voice within the air above.

Raising my eyes from the caressing flowers,
    I saw a bird; 'twas singing high aloft;
Fair bird with golden feathers, and a voice
    No mortal ever heard, more wondrous clear and soft.
It sang and sang beneath the cloudless sky;
    A world of melody, of wild and rapturous glee;
And with its eyes soft glancing down in mine,
    I knew the bird was singing, but for me.

No sparkling wine, no gladdening nectar ere,
    Had power to thrill, as did each liquid tone;
It flowed into my very heart, and soul,
    'Till they grew wild and lived for that alone.
I did not live, existed but entranced,
    Lost in the transports deep, their sweetness lent,
The wild rare rapture of the birdling's song,
    The flowers' bright hue, and deep exquisite scent.

In 'midst of bliss, o'er smiling sky there came
    A deep dark mass, a sullen cloud of gray,
That hid the blue, and then loud crashed and broke,
    Falling in torrents on my flowers gay.
Bright blossoms, ah, they lay around me crushed;
    Both life and fragrance from their hearts had fled.
And woe! the birdling's voice grew strangely still,
    Poised in his golden beauty o'er my head.

A flash of lightning 'cross the heavens speed,
    I feared its course, and loud in terror cried:

Too late! the fire had cleft the bird of life.
  It swiftly fell, and in my bosom died.
Wild with regret I sorrowed o'er its form
  And shed hot tears, upon each flower's face,
Nor cared the rain was chilling soul, and heart,
  Nor noted blackness filled once smiling space.

*　*　*　*　*　*　*　*

Like some spent thought the thunder ceased, its din,
  The clouds surrendered to the smiling sky,
Some few new flowers sprang from the moistened earth,
  But still and cold my singing bird did lie.
With the fresh breath the new spring flowers did wave,
  More tranquil grew my heart from its wild grief
Though joy and happiness together fled,
  The new-born fragrance brought some blessed relief.

In dull cold apathy, with flowers crushed
  The singing bird low lying at my feet.
Reclined I on the flowers' bed of death,
  That late with happiness had been replete.
My only pleasure now the scattered leaves,
  My eyes fixed ever on the lifeless form
Of the bright bird, my own sweet singing bird
  I mourned and sighed for their lost golden charm.

Soft as the flutter of a fair rose-leaf,
  Upon some moss within a wooded wild,
I heard a sound creep vaguely through the air,
  Sweet as the breathing of a sleeping child.
Half sullenly I raised my tear-wet eyes,
  Ah me! to greet so wondrous pure a sight,
For where the golden bird had poised and sung,
  Now flashed a dove so gentle and so white.

Deep in my heart reflected was its breast,
 Its mild dear eyes, its gleaming wings of snow,
Like moonlight smiling with a tender grace,
 Or starlight's chastened silver glow.
The voice swelled not in sweet delicious song
 As did the bird now dead, but ah! my mind
Was lulled to quiet and my o'er-tired heart,
 From its low tones repose, and rest did find.

Still in my dream I woke, the dove did lie,
 With furled white wings, close o'er my heart and breast,
Its whisperings bearing such a holy calm,
 Its gleaming purity swift flashing rest.
I kissed its form and called it gentle Peace,
 It pleased me so to call it by this name,
When 'neath its spell of holy restful calm,
 More near to God it seemed my spirit came.

Just then your voice dispelled my vivid dream,
 Ah would thou'dst, sweet, in resting let me stay,
For back again to tangled thread of life,
 My dream and dove did vanish both away,
Sweet one, thou knowest it was only dream
 Of waking, that I tell now unto you.
A vague dim history of my own heart-life,
 That floats in retrospect before my view.

Ah, the sweet rest in Love's enchanted land,
 Ah, the bright singing of Love's golden bird
And oh, the anguish of the cloudy fate,
 Whose rain and blackness could not be deferred;
Then the new springing of Hope's gentle flowers,
 And the dear coming of the Dove of Peace.

There was unrest e'en n the gold bird's joy,
    But the white dove made all unquiet cease.

Each has its charm. but one is holier far,
    The one thou knowest of the snow-like gleam ;
But see the sun is creeping in my room,
    'Tis time to live, and time to cease to dream.

SEPARATION.*

YOUR face it is with me everywhere,
    In the sky, in the stars, in the perfumed air.
In the rose that I clasp, in the book I hold,
In the silence of night, in the day of gold.

Your eyes, but they haunt me always dear,
In my doubt, in my joy, in my hope and fear,
They are meeting mine own in their liquid light,
Be it dazzling day, be it darksome night.

Your face, and your eyes, how they glow and shine,
In their wonderful depths looking back into mine,
And oh, the pity, and oh, the pain,
That they haunt me ever, and all in vain.

For the story is writ, and must be my own,
That my life pass on in its monotone,
For the story is writ, and ever must be ;
You are nothing to me, you are nothing to me.

---

* Perhaps the last poetic production of her pen. Received by editor
"Woman's Tribune," Washington, D. C., just before the author's
death, and published after.

Nothing to me, yet my God how much!
I would die for the joy of your mouth's sweet touch.
I would count life little in your caress,
And God's best gift, if that love He'd bless.

The clasp of your hand is Heaven, my own,
Yet loving you thus, I must be alone,
And the bitterest pain of all is this,
That I never may know your caress or kiss.

And the bitterest part that Love's wild, deep song,
Were it answered dear, it were wrong, 'twere wrong.
For duty and life and all decree,
You can, and you must be nothing to me.

Yet I love you living, I'll love you e'er,
I would rather love you in life's despair,
Than any one else 'neath the smiling sky,
So you knew that I loved you, and felt my sigh.

And oh, the pity, and oh, the pain,
That our love must be like a lost refrain.
But your face, oh, it haunts me everywhere,
In my work, in my song, in my thought and prayer.

And so it is dear, and ever must be,
And yet you are nothing, oh, nothing to me.
Nothing, yet all, and everything, dear,
For love springeth out of doubting, and fear.

In this world I must bear it alone — alone,
In the tragic waste of my monotone.
But in Heaven, I pray that God will decree,
My darling at last may be something to me.

www.ingramcontent.com/pod-product-compliance
Lightning Source LLC
Chambersburg PA
CBHW030828270326
41928CB00007B/944